Dedicated to all those, who
are puzzled by an Indian
around them.

Copyright © Sharad Awasthi, 2015

The moral right of the author has been asserted
All rights reserved

Without limiting the rights under copyright reserved above, no part of this publication may be reproduced into a retrieval system, or transmitted, in any form or by any means (electronic, mechanical, photocopying, recording or otherwise), without the prior written permission of both the copyright owner and the publisher of this book.

Contents

Preface 8

Introduction 11

A 13

Arranged Marriage 14

Auto Rickshaw ride 17

B 20

Body Language 21

    Greeting - To touch, kiss or not? 21

    Cross-talking 21

    No Left Hand 22

    Nose-picking 23

    No feet please 23

    Eating with the mouth open 24

    Drinking with a slurp 24

    Judged by plentiful parameters 24

    Yawning and Sneezing with God's name 25

    Starting the sentence with "No" 25

    Confused Middle finger 26

    The great Indian 'YES' nod 27

BAJAJ® Scooter 29

Books 29

C 31

5 'C's of India – Essential 32

    1st C - Cinema 32

2nd C - Cricket 38

3rd C - Congress..41

4th C – Corruption...42

5th C - Caste system..45

Cleaning our Homes 47

Cycles are for the poor 49

Corporate Indians – Grownup Kids 50

D...53

Date of Birth – Many 54

Driving in India..55

Drinking Means Drunk...58

E...60

Exit – Missing the Knowhow 61

Eating Style...63

F...66

Foreign Travel...67

Fair Complexion Attracts..69

G...72

Guests are God..73

Gold Means Everything 75

H...77

Humor 78

Holidays – An Indian Meaning 78

I..81

A-Z Dealing with Indians

Indian Railways - everyone owns them 83

J 91

Jugaad – Making Things Work 92

K 94

Know It All – Only Superficially 95

Kite Flying – Not Dreams... 96

L 98

Law Breaking 99

Living with Parents 100

Living with In-Laws 101

Lifestyle 102

    Pronunciation 102

    From Stranger to Extended Family 103

    Time Management 104

    Thrifty, not miser 105

    Superstition 105

    No Sorry, Thank You or Please 107

    Handling embarrassment 107

    Daily Newspaper 107

    Idea of Hitler 108

    Conversations and Compliments 109

    Others 109

M 111

Marriage as Festival 112

    Marriage Procession: 113

Nagin Dance 115
The Marriage itself 116
The role of different family members 117
After Marriage 118
Maids and Helpers 119
Mobile Phones 121
Mahatma Gandhi 124
Modernity and Development Redefined 125
Medical System 127
N 130
Names of Indians 131
Non Resident Indians (NRIs) 132
O 134
Obsession with Tea & Coffee 135
Office Meetings 137
Old Age & Retirement Homes 138
P 141
Parenting - Never-ending 142
Privacy 145
Philosophies of an Indians 147
Trust: 147
Pride: 149
Honor and Respect: 151
Fate: 154

Status: 154

Help: 155

Sharm or Haya: 155

Karma and Seven Lives: 156

Q 158

Quotient of Colors 159

R 161

Relatives and Relationships 162

List of named relationships: 163

Rakhi 164

Karvachauth 165

Religions 166

Restaurants 173

Reaching India 177

Roadside Assistance 178

Spiritual Chanting and Home Temples 181

Schools 183

Safety is for Dumb, to Secure is Smartness 186

T 189

Toilets 190

Travel Scams & Safe Travel 191

U 193

Union of Indian States 194

USA is aped - Britain is disliked 196

V 198

Vegetarianism 199
Villages 204
W 206
Women Dressing 207
Work Culture – Chalta Hai 209
Weather and Time Zone 211
X 214
Xclusive Shopping List for foreigners 215
Y 216
Yoga 217
Z 219
Zoo – We live here 220

Preface

Why do Indians fail to say 'No'?
What does 'left hand' mean to an Indian?
Where is privacy in India?
Why can't they eat beef?
What is arranged marriage?
When can an Indian be addressed with first name?

Often same questions about Indians, living abroad also bewilder many. While Indians living abroad not only look different, they do act differently too. They also make unintentional mistakes, which could be perfectly appropriate in India.

In Indian culture, the smallest acceptable gesture of gratitude to a stranger is to offer him or her tea or coffee. If invited to one's home, it is the least expected. Usually, people insist because first offer is considered mandatory and second offer makes it sincere. On this occasion, I offered coffee to a German female colleague of mine, as a gratitude for dropping me home in her car. As Indian culture naturally directed me, I made a second offer and insisted. Apparently, the reaction was cold. In the days to follow, our working relationship became colder. It was only after living in Germany for some time that I understood my unintentional mistake. Offering coffee does not necessarily mean 'coffee'!

'A-Z Dealing with Indians – A Secret Guide' will help those traveling to India, or interacting with Indians, found elsewhere in the world. There are many tips and tricks suggested in the book to help you sail smoothly through India's cultural diversity and the hidden contradictions with cultures outside India. This book will definitely prevent the readers from making unintentional cultural blunders.

In order to be effective and efficient, when dealing with Indians around you, wherever and whenever, it is important to know why Indians do things, the way they do. Being Indian, like any other nationals, is a process of thoughts and habits, cultivated over a long period of time. This book is about the construct of an Indian national psyche. It is made of various facets of how Indians think, learn and do things, wherever they are living. Although there are many sources of information about India and Indian culture, this book will connect those dry facts to comprehensively compose the traits of 'The Indians'.

I have attempted to simplify the topics in order to depict a generic mindset shared by all Indians.

Travel guides are about places. 'A-Z Dealing with Indians' is about the people of India. The use of this book is not necessarily restricted to travelers visiting India for pleasure or for business. It is also useful for groups who work with Indian team members or corporations with Indian employees.

I was born and brought up in India and have traveled to many countries and continents for business and leisure. In the last decade or so, I have experienced and resolved many corporate challenges, minor and substantial, arising from cultural misunderstandings due to conflicting expectations. This experience has prompted me to attempt writing this guide, to enable people, better understand Indians.

My aim is to provide an everlasting asset for travelers and businesses across the globe. I hope that readers will find it useful.

☺

Sharad Awasthi

contact@sharadawasthi.com

Facebook:

https://www.facebook.com/AtoZDealingwithIndians/

Acknowledgements

Thank you India, for providing a source of diversity that is found nowhere else in the world. It is a cradle of civilization and culture with aspects that are fundamental to human beings. Hope India continues to hold on to the rich traditions and practices that have defined it for more than 5000 years.

Thank you to more than a billion Indians, in India and abroad, for providing me with examples of your characteristic behavior. Your thoughts, words and deeds have helped me to understand the human geography of each region of India. Though these features together make a billion Indian lives, still you are all unique. It is a feat in itself.

Thank you to my parents, for being Indian and making me part of this outstanding nation. Without being born there, it would have been very difficult to grasp the essence of being an Indian.

Thank you to my wife, Anupama, for supporting me financially. While I was describing the nature of Indians in words, you helped me edit my work and sharpen my descriptions of the Indian life. You have brought a significant improvement to my work with your keen cultural observations and numerous lengthy discussions.

Thank you to my non-Indian friends, for posing so many questions about Indians that have puzzled you for a long time. I hope this book will provide answers to most of them. It was just after I started writing that I realized how baffling Indian behavior can be. Understanding an Indian seems to be a complex matter.

Apologies to anybody, if my expressed views have caused inconvenience to a person, community, religion, organization or nation. It was purely unintentional, though. It is my aim to be polite and humorous.

Thank you to all those readers who have shown interest in India and Indians, by way of tourism, business and constant curiosity.

Introduction

India is flourishing today, an attractive destination for both tourism and commercial enterprise. Every year, millions flock to achieve their goals and they all want to know much more than the usual travel guides. Millions in the world have Indian colleagues in their organizations, and tourists from India explore local streets of the world. Since India is culturally very different from other societies of the world, so are its people. Hence, interacting with Indians can become a very tricky and challenging experience.

Often, small mistakes are made during an intercultural interaction, which could be crucial to a large business deal, a friendship or a loving relationship. These mistakes are usually unintentional, but when words or actions have different cultural interpretations, they can lead to a blunder. Let me cite a simple example. It is common in the west for people working in an office to put their feet on the table. There are widely-used pictures of US presidents doing this. For an Indian, anybody doing this in office or home is highly offensive and just this little body posture might even break a deal.

It is a usual complaint from my friends in the west that Indians never give "No" for an answer. Even for a Herculean task, the answer is always positive, though not necessarily affirmative. Over-commitment is not the individual's problem, but a national inability to refuse outright that comes from an Indian culture.

Many aspects interplay that define an Indian reasoning, such as the treatment of guests in India, the rules of driving, vegetarianism, religion and honor, dress code, body language, etc. All of these are potential blind spots, so it is worthwhile developing an insight into an Indian reasoning.

Any country's culture is extensive and could take a lifetime to understand. As of now India has twenty-nine states. Now imagine getting to know the culture of twenty-nine different countries to formulate your interaction with Indians. It will be a mammoth undertaking. At your workplace, there could be Indians from any of the twenty-nine different states of India.

A great solution to these challenges of interacting successfully with Indians is to learn about the common factors that have defined and shaped their 'Indian' persona, within India or elsewhere.

The book is alphabetically arranged by topics which matter most according to an Indian. They are necessarily not in the order of priority, instead they all are important.

The tips and tricks suggested in this book will help readers navigate through these aspects and readers for themselves will be able to derive the key differences from other cultures. In today's world of high mobility and interconnectedness interacting with Indians is often a necessity, so why not make it an enjoyable and productive experience?

A

- Arranged Marriage
- Auto Rickshaw Ride

Arranged Marriage

Arranged marriage is an interesting aspect of life in India. It is common to many religions and is a feature of Hinduism, Islam, Sikhism and some Christian sects. The girl and the boy do not find each other or decide themselves to get married; their families do it on their behalf. Until recently, it was common for a member of the family to stride up to the boy and joyfully announce that his marriage has been arranged. More remarkable than this is the boy's and girl's acceptance of their prospective spouse, without having met each other.

The search for a suitable match could be done through an advertisement in the matrimonial columns of a newspaper, or an internet search on matrimonial websites, or by word of mouth through friends, relatives and neighbors. People look for matches within their community, so usually it is done by word of mouth. On weekends, there are additional pages in the national and local newspapers advertising brides and grooms. The matches are classified according to community, religion or caste. Beyond that, there are no strict criteria for a suitable match. The descriptions mention broad guidelines such as 'good family', 'good education', 'good income', or they specify a profession such as a doctor or engineer.

In the hierarchy of professions, those most highly regarded are medical doctor, civil servant and an engineer. Next in line would be a chartered accountant. Other professions are considered to be a compromise or a substitute for those who failed to make it into medicine or engineering. This viewpoint is boldly reflected in the Indian society. There is pride in the voice and a sparkle in the eyes of an Indian who is introduced as an engineer or a medical doctor.

In some communities, there are also periodic community meetings and wedding fairs to facilitate the arranged marriage. The parents bring along their sons and daughters to find a suitable match. A typical gathering has more than hundred families. Like the job fair, all are required to submit a one-page profile to the organizers. Also, the families are given an opportunity to take the stage to present their profile and expectations. Based on these profiles, the families then choose to meet in person in breakout sessions. The expectations discussed in this private meeting are about the details of job, travel and relocation plans, cooking skills, health issues, income levels, location of stay, slimming and trimming requirements (if), timelines for making babies and other issues of living in a joint family system. The parents then shortlist the prospective matches based on the meeting. The fair also provides services for palmistry, horoscope matching and professional portfolio photography.

> **In the hierarchy of professions, most highly regarded are medical doctors, civil servants and engineers.**

When a suitable match is found, who meets the parents' criteria, the boy's family visits the girl's house. The boy also accompanies his parents to visit his prospective bride. Usually a high tea is served to the guests by the girl's family. More lavish the food is, higher the respect is shown by the girl's family. It is worth noting that this stage comes only when profile pictures are exchanged and accepted by both families, and have subsequently approved them. The visit indicates a 50% chance of a match being finalized. Quite often, the talk about marriage does not proceed further simply because the girl did not look as beautiful as in the picture!

The two families talk to each other at this meeting and ask investigative questions to establish whether this is the right match for the future of the combined family. The girl and the boy have no role to play in this process. They are like spectators at a tennis match, waiting to cheer themselves as winners. The parents on both sides decide whether to go ahead or not.

The criteria of match making are as follows, listed in the order of priority along with the chance of it being negotiated:

1. Religion – Only 1% chance of a compromise
2. Caste and Community – Only 5% chance of a compromise

3. Horoscope – 50% chance of a compromise

4. Age – Only 5% chance of a compromise

5. Professional Status and income – 75% chance of a compromise

6. Physical appearance – 99% chance of a compromise

Usually, the girl and the boy are able to talk to each other at this meeting, although it is very formal. Some consider it a bit modern, but nowadays, in big cities, they do actually talk to each other multiple times, or even go out for dinner. This is a very long way from what is considered as a date in the west, though they do ask personal questions about topics ranging from hobbies and family size to favorite foods or movies. At the next stage, if the parents get on well, they would clearly say "yes". It has to be spoken aloud, clearly and definitively for the formalization of the relationship. There may or may not be a decision on the date of the formal engagement at this point, but families do exchange token gifts (usually a piece of gold jewelry) to mark this occasion of formalization.

The girl and the boy are not consulted about a marriage date in most cases. Usually it is planned for some auspicious day advised by the families' priests. The family's priest in most cases also doubles as an astrologer. Also, the marriage date is fixed by the parents after consulting their senior relatives and avoiding any possible clash with another family wedding. Weddings happen during a season, according to the Hindu calendar. So on a particularly auspicious day there could be 15,000 to 18,000 marriages in a city like Delhi alone. In many cases, there could be more than one wedding on that day in a large family.

The guest list and the gifts to be exchanged are arranged, like everything else, by the parents on both sides. The venue and the arrangements for the wedding are decided by the girl's parents and approved by the boy's parents. This is to ensure that social status is considered and the plan suits guests who are going to arrive with boosted egos. It is about showing off by the boy's parents about the 'worth' of their son.

There is nothing like a pre-nuptial agreement in Hindu marriages. Although Islam provides for compensation, declared by the priest at the time of formalizing the marriage. It is more of a religious ritual. Certainly, in either case, solicitors are not required to be part of the marriage in any way.

This is arranged marriage, in all its practices and perspectives.

99% of the Indian marriages last forever.

For the day of the marriage, everything is arranged for the boy and the girl. They just have to dress up and be present at dozens of ceremonies lasting five to seven days. On the emotional front, it all starts with the celebrations and festivities. The emotional attachment between the bride and groom is not expected to happen before marriage. It is assumed that things really will work, and compatibility is not discussed at all. Falling in love begins after the wedding!

Interestingly the couple, who have met each other for just a few hours and seldom talked to each other alone, consummate their relationship on the night of the wedding. It is called *Suhaag Raat*, or 'husband's night'. To the westerners this is unimaginable, but it is true in India. As strange as this arranged marriage sounds, it does work, with an apparently higher success rate than in the west. Ninety-nine percent of marriages in India, last forever.

Auto Rickshaw ride

If there is something that has caught the imagination of Indian automobile manufacturers, it must be the auto rickshaw. It is neither a motor bike with pillion rider nor a car with a steering wheel. Yet it carries up to six or eight passengers on a tiny 200 cc engine. There are a few millions of them on the country roads, successfully solving the problem of public transport across the Indian landscape. This great Indian masterpiece combines the features of the car, the motorbike, the cab and the bus. It plies its trade between personal destinations and on official routes.

In a car, you have a seat belt, which is absent in the auto rickshaw, and it is also missing a door. The cover is canvas stretched like a tent and the wiper is not motorized. The driver moves it manually. There are side indicators, but they are not used; instead hand signals are preferred. The informal and helpful behavior of the Indian passenger comes spontaneously handy when a passenger gives a hand signal on the driver's behalf. In any case, it does not matter much even if there was a signal or not when an auto rickshaw is turning. All Indians are extraordinarily alert and proactive when negotiating the roads. Moreover, the auto drivers are a breed apart who have developed a sixth sense when maneuvering through the narrowest of lanes, and negotiating the smallest spaces in between the congested traffic.

The windscreen of an auto rickshaw is filled with stickers, pictures and decorations featuring movie stars and the Gods, making you wonder how the driver can see through it. But there is nothing to worry about, because there is a horn, which chases away all dangers. It is very sharp, used with shrieking volleys, so that not only the intended recipient is alerted but also the adjoining neighborhood too. Everyone in the vicinity detests the fact that this three-wheeled vehicle is near them. It is more of a constant irritant than an alert to keep clear of its way.

Auto rickshaw services are available for all the purposes that taxis and buses would fulfill. Like a bus service, it might be used for passengers traveling from point to point on a pre-defined route. Or like a taxi, you can hire the entire auto for yourself to reach a destination.

Either way, you can decide on the place where you want to disembark. Just tap on the driver's shoulder and he will do the courtesy of dropping you off.

It is a once in a lifetime experience to ride an auto rickshaw in India. Journey to India is incomplete without it.

You could call it a motorbike, as it has just one headlight, though the luminosity is no more than a burning candle. But the six or eight pillion riders, sitting in rows as in a car, contradict that classification. Like a motor bike, the driver has handlebars to steer, unlike the car with its steering wheel. Also, there is no central gear stick. Instead, the gears are on the handlebars.

Payments are by cash only, and you can haggle over the fare every time you step in this great Indian innovation.

The advantage of riding the auto is its maneuverability. It is used effectively by drivers at traffic lights to squeeze into the gap between two bumpers. The advantage of grabbing these inches of space helps passengers immensely when navigating the clogged Indian city roads.

Indians love to get on the transport rapidly. They get highly impatient if the wait to board the public transport is substantial. Once on board, like the other traffic, they can move at a snail's pace, which is acceptable. This propensity of 'get things now' comes with great ease in India. There are auto rickshaws in every nook and corner, their driver scanning every passer-by while waiting for a passenger. Just an eye contact with the driver and this chauffeur driven three wheelers, will be at your service.

> **Indians find it hard to wait, and have little patience, when seeking a service.**

B

- Body Language
- BAJAJ® Scooter
- Books

Body Language

The core of understanding a culture lies in understanding the body language of its people. Even though India has a huge landscape and incorporates a variety of religions, cultures, traditions and communities, generic body language more or less defines their Indian-ness. Generally, it is very informal and does not follow classical western style etiquettes. Indians have their own Do's and Don'ts that are strictly followed.

Greeting - To touch, kiss or not?

Friends, especially male friends, commonly touch each other and put their arms around the shoulder (as soccer team players do). They also can share rides on a two-wheeler. They shake hands and often embrace each other. Womenfolk can also embrace each other or shake hands. Generally, in India, men and women do not touch each other even by way of a greeting. They might touch the feet of a senior of the opposite sex, but that is more of a respectful gesture. Instead, people greet the opposite sex with folded hands, called *Namaste*. Since a large population is also Muslim, it will help if greeted by *Adaab*.

Only children can be kissed in public. Adult kissing in public, especially a French kiss, will attract serious objection. There are many self-proclaimed moral policemen who will walk up to you to convey their objection, and might even create a scene. Kissing, when meeting each other is not the Indian way. It is accepted when meeting children, and if possible, infants are taken in the arms, like loving parents would do.

Cross-talking

When in an Indian's company, one should be prepared to be part of cross talking. Most Indians, if they are not listening to a spiritual leader on a dais, love to cut short your sentences and speak out of turn. If they are not able to do so, they get very restless and that might be indicated in their body language. If the other person still does not stop talking, there could be parallel talking for minutes.

When Indians communicate over the phone, if not cross talking, they will definitely be doing something in parallel. This might mean that they are giving non-verbal instructions to someone else in the room, while talking to you on the phone. One should not be surprised if something irrelevant to the discussion is heard from an Indian caller. This is an instruction to someone else that you will also hear. Do not expect this instruction to begin with an apology or an excuse. Expect to be puzzled as to how that part of the sentence was related to the ongoing conversation. Only later with some guess work would you realize that it was not intended for you. It is better to ignore that part of your conversation, as this syndrome of additional talk on the phone is common with Indians.

Most conversations in India is Informal, even in the business meetings.

Indian TV journalists are best at cross-talking on national shows. They aren't only interrupting; they also do not apologize for the intrusion. It is a habit which is a typical characteristic of the TV journalist. There are a couple of reasons for doing it. One, they have the microphone so they can remove it from the speaker whenever they want to speak themselves, and secondly, like most 'know it all' Indians, they already know the argument, after only a few words have been spoken. In one instance, a TV journalist was considered so overbearing that he was said to be a man-made wonder like the Great Wall of China, because he could be heard from space. The unspoken rule of TV shows stipulates 'my show, my voice'.

No Left Hand

An Indian body is half dirty and half pure. The left hand is considered an inauspicious hand and can bring dishonor if not used appropriately. This is because the left hand is the 'potty hand' and is used for washing after going to the toilet. Hence, anything which is honorable or auspicious must be done with the right hand. Up until recently, and maybe still a practice in rural areas, children born left-handed are purposefully trained to use the right hand. Using the left might get those children punished.

Although most schools do not discriminate children, with either hand being used, in the social life of India, transacting cash with the left hand is a no-go. Serving or eating food with left hand will attract the wrong kind of attention. Gifts are not given with left hand neither is offerings to God. While conducting a prayer service, no act is primarily done with the left hand, at most, it can be an assisting hand.

When dealing with Indians, please avoid the left hand as much as possible.

Nose-picking

Nose-picking when someone facing you is quite possible in India. Even if you are looking in the eyes of the person, he/she will still finish the job. Once it has been dug out, it is rolled into small balls using index finger and thumb and then dropped on the floor. If it is the host's house, it could well be stuck under the bed or on the side of the sofa or anywhere else. Do not expect apologies, since it is not a mistake, but rather a deliberate act of cleaning up.

Similarly, Indians (especially the elderly) might insert their little finger into their ears and give it a nice long poke, while talking to you. They can also be seen using the arm of their spectacles for the job. This is to give a nice scratch to the inside of the ear to remove nature's produce. The instrument is not cleaned or wiped afterwards.

What it comes down to, is that people from different countries or places have different definitions of 'hygiene'. One cannot argue any further. If you do, prepare to be ridiculed for being cleaner than it is necessary.

No feet please

It is a conundrum of Indian society. On one hand touching someone's feet is considered as a way of taking blessings, on the other hand the feet are not considered to be a part of the body that should be touched or shown to anyone. The only time when the feet are used is to disrespect someone in the worst possible way. Laying your feet on the table or pointing them towards another person is considered utter disrespect and is a guaranteed formula to break a relationship.

In case, someone unintentionally touches someone with his feet, whether walking, standing, sitting or changing postures, it becomes compulsory to seek sincerest of apologies. Failure to do so will attract negative response and objection. If the other person is a stranger, be prepared to take an abuse. When the Mumbai local trains run packed with thrice or four times its capacity, passengers might push or squeeze them to make space, but simultaneously make an earnest attempt to not touch anything else with their feet. This may be someone else's bag or feet itself.

All foot wears are also considered as derogatory. Therefore, any simile with footwear has demeaning connotation. It is a practice in all Indian homes to remove footwear before entering the kitchen. Many Indians, in India and abroad also practice removing footwear before entering the house. Though footwear is allowed in the churches all over the world, all other religions followed in India strictly prohibit footwear in the temple premises. In fact, as a gesture to seek an apology and express regret, members of Sikh community polish the footwear of the pilgrims at the Sikh temples.

Eating with the mouth open
When the bite of food enters the Indian mouth, it can be seen by others in the room during its grinding. All the chewing takes place in full public glare. As saliva gets added, a loud sound can be heard which resembles the sound of batter mixing in a bowl. If you don't like it, it is better to switch on some background music to mask the sound of mastication.

Drinking with a slurp
If you hear a deep sound like that of a steam railway engine, watch out for an Indian in the vicinity, enjoying a hot drink. Whether it is tea or milk or coffee, any hot drink goes in with a loud slurp. You can count it as, one sip, one slurp. If one would like to know why they slurp rather than drink quietly, the answer will be about the divine sense of taste that comes with a deep slurp. Indians have a reason for doing everything.

Judged by plentiful parameters
Unlike the western society, where mostly a person is judged on the basis of education, experience, personal stories, credentials, in India, there are plenteous other parameters used to judge a person. It could be the color of his/her hair, the clothes he/she wears, the way he/she sits, the way they talk, the quantity they talk, the topics they have an opinion on,

the place where they live, the kind of house they have, the model of car they drive, etc. For example, it is a good chance, if an Indian living outside the country, is assumed to be drinking lots of alcohol every day. It is a natural assumption that they would be ignoring their families back in India, would be arrogant, unaware of things happening in India and be least religious and unfaithful in following the traditions. Also, they would be wearing only the formal cocktail dresses.

Why? Judging puts Indians in control and command. It's a latent need. For them it is like having the steering wheel of the situation in their hands.

Indians can judge communities and people they have never met before and about which they know little. Once a community or religion or person has been judged, it gets type cast and the chances of reversing the opinion are very slim. No further information, credentials, facts, debates or even research papers can prove otherwise. Hence, it is comfortable to assume the Indian opinion as the final verdict.

Yawning and Sneezing with God's name

Indians remember God all the time. That is why Indians always call the name of their favorite God or just say "Hey Bhagwan" (meaning "Oh God") while yawning or sneezing. If the Gods were to respond each time they were summoned, they would constantly be handling calls from India's 1.2 billion population. The rest of the world would be neglected. God help the world!

Starting the sentence with "No"

"No" means "No" – well, most of the time. Each response in a conversation starts with "No" when talking to an Indian. Do not be bamboozled, this is normal. You say it should be 'A', the Indian response will be about 'B'. You say it should be 'B', the Indian response will be 'A'. This is normal. They have to disagree with the other person most of the time, in order to prove that they are more knowledgeable than others. And it is not just one single "No" used as prefix to every sentence; it is at least three or four consequent ones in a rhythm. It could even be more if the idea is to show how far they disagree with your comment/argument.

Confused Middle finger

It would have been a normal practice to use the index finger to point things out. But with the process of strengthening the morals, the schools also teach children about "not pointing one's fingers at someone else". Metaphorically, it is also engrained, that pointing at someone makes three other folded fingers point it back at you. Hence, those who are conscious of holding their morals upright, are also confused when using their index finger. It leaves the option of using the thumb, the ring finger or the little finger to point things out.

As a body language in India, the thumb is mostly sarcastic. Also, the Indian government has a role to play here. The officials use thumb impression for citizens who are illiterate, unable to do their signatures, leave alone read any language. Publicly displaying a thumb is a sign of being illiterate. Also, waving a thumb with closed fist is a gesture of saying "get lost".

An educated Indian mind is not designed to agree with anyone or anything else. Showing the little finger, though cute, means that an Indian needs a tinkle. So the little finger does not stand a chance of performing the all-important task of pointing at things.

It leaves the ring finger to be the pointer. Unfortunately, the mechanics of the palm does not allow the ring finger to stand alone efficiently. It does well only when other fingers are standing tall by its side.

For Indians, this leaves only the middle finger to do the honors.

When an Indian uses the middle finger, it is not to abuse. Looking at the hands closely, isn't the middle finger the longest one? So the middle finger takes the point closer to the object making it the favorite finger when pointing. So the Indians show the middle finger at everything, whether their computer screens, a piece of paper, corporate presentations or the moon in the sky.

Although it would be incorrect to say that the Indians might not understand the meaning of the middle finger, there are enough Hollywood movies to demonstrate its meaning well.

The great Indian 'YES' nod

The 'Yes' nod

It may not look like a complete 'Yes' nor an emphatic 'No'. The Indian Yes nod means "I heard you". It does not mean agreement. Therefore, it is important to confirm whether it is in agreement or not.

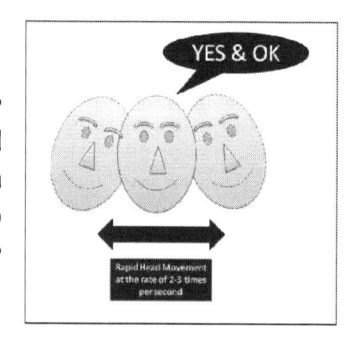

Instead of verbally asking a fellow Indian about their well-being, it is the usual practice to communicate with facial gestures. So, "what's going on?" will be asked by raising the eyebrows along with a slight upward jerk to the face, accompanied with a smile.

Indians rarely say "No". If they do, it is an event. So is the facial expression. A blank expression without any nod or movement is an acceptable way to mean "No" for an answer.

Like other communications using facial expressions, annoyance is expressed with a facial jerk on one side.

Calling someone closer to talk, especially when annoyed, is expressed by a facial jerk in a downward direction. This will indicate to the other Indian that a more powerful one has called. Bigger the frown, harsher will be the consequence.

BAJAJ® Scooter

As the story goes, once NASA® was facing difficulty launching a rocket. They checked all the parameters and even ignited the engine, yet the rocket would not budge. As usual, the problem was reported to an Indian. It was a quick and easy solution, as if written on the back of his hand. He suggested tilting the rocket once to the left, and a few seconds later to the right. Then he ignited the rocket and off went NASA's spacecraft into orbit. Later at the press conference, much was discussed about the intuitive and innovative way an Indian had launched NASA's immobile piece of engineering. The answer lies back home in India, where millions daily solve the problem of malfunctioning automobiles.

Like the NASA rocket in the story, the driver tilts the BAJAJ two-wheeler on either side for a couple of seconds each, and off it goes with a single kick. Never in the history of the automobile has the problem been so ingeniously solved. There are millions of BAJAJ scooters plying the Indian roads and every morning their proud owners make use of this trick. Though made in different years as various models, those million owners have just this unique solution for a scooter that does not crank.

Books

Books have a very poor market in India. Textbooks are the only books, most Indians like to read, as it is strictly related to their syllabus and academic curriculum. Anything beyond the curriculum is considered superfluous and hence a waste of time. Reading for pleasure is not very prevalent, except for people with special interest.

Corporate India is typical. If you are a manager, even with a small team of five members, there will have to be a set of self-help, motivational and management books displayed in an appropriate place. Airports are the key places to buy these "display books". Only if everything said in those books were read by them, corporate India would be spinning gold.

It is not the fault of publishers that there are not many books published in India; it is that people are less literate and impatient to read a book from cover to cover. The political and social content are covered in newspapers along with gossips from Bollywood and seems to be enough to satisfy their literary appetite. This does not mean that newspapers and magazines are a source of literary genius. Though newspapers are seen as a good read, but I doubt if people reach the page with editorial columns after scanning the headlines and the page 3 gossips. Also, most of the reputed newspapers are turning into tabloids.

Indians prefer magazines to formal books. It can be inferred that Indians prefer images and visuals than reading boring plain text in the books. You could also conclude that Indian society is more influenced by movie theatres than libraries. Every town has at least a dozen movie theatres, but finding a library is like a treasure hunt.

Generally, Indians are an instinctive lot. They don't need to read thoroughly to get the essence. They just get the gist of things and the rest of the message is reconstructed. In India this is called 'getting an idea'. Similarly, for every task that an Indian like to perform, they first want to 'get an idea' before setting foot into the mud.

Indians are generally poor readers because their source of knowledge and entertainment is by talking to fellow Indians. Within a few minutes, any two Indians get engaged in deep conversations about topics of general interest, asking questions, seeking opinion, sharing experiences of self and their acquaintances, giving advice and facilitating recommendations.

They consider that knowledge from word-of-mouth is the most authentic. Similarly, Indians want to gossip as part of their entertainment, which they do so either by visiting each other's homes or over mobiles. Given a choice, they would like to talk even to strangers than sit tight in a corner with an exciting book.

C

- 5'C's of India – Essential
  - ➢ 1st C - Cinema
  - ➢ 2nd C - Cricket
  - ➢ 3rd C – Congress
  - ➢ 4th C – Corruption
  - ➢ 5th C - Caste system
- Cleaning our Homes
- Cycles are for Poor
- Corporate Indians – Grownup Kids

5 'C's of India – Essential

1st C - Cinema

The lives of Indians revolve around cinema and movies. The cinema theaters are also called 'talkies' in general parlance. There is a background that explains why Indians love and would almost die for Indian cinema. After India's independence in 1947, there was hardly any infrastructure for entertainment. All that was available in the country were a few cinema theaters. When people could not afford air conditioning, during the hot summers, a good three hours in a cool cinema hall were a respite for many, of course along with entertainment.

The craze for Indian cinema and actors began in early 30s. As time went on, the demand for more cinemas increased because the industry was selling dreams and entertainment to an impoverished nation. A major factor that promoted the dreams offered by movies was the disparity between on-screen fantasy and off-screen society. Off-screen society was poor, traditional and conservative, lived out in congested huts and small houses. On-screen, life was glamorous and modern, with characters indulging in love affairs, driving large American cars, running around trees and flowers, singing and celebrating their joyous life out in the open.

In movies from the 1960s and 1970s, the portrayal of romance was symbolic, such as lovers drinking with two straws from same coconut, drenching under one umbrella, couple running on the sea shore (in slow motion) or two flowers kissing and swaying in a light breeze. That was the era when romance in a conservative society was being sold to Indians through the silver screen. I would say 99% of the movies were about love affairs and romance, like poor man's Indian Mills and Boon® stories.

This period is considered as "the golden age" of Indian cinema. The actors and actresses gained larger-than-life status and the Indians would do any crazy thing to get their attention. Young girls even wrote letters with their blood to express admiration and love for their silver screen idols.

The defining moment exhibiting craze for the Indian cinema came in the 1980s. One of the leading superstars, Amitabh Bachchan, was accidentally injured while shooting a movie. It was a life-threatening injury, involving another, lesser-known co-artist. As the news broke of the accident, the nation came to a grinding halt. The national news media, newspapers and the TV channel (there was only one), repeatedly reported the incident as a headline.

This would sound like overkill in today's short lifespan of news items. The streets reverberated with prayers as millions went to the temples and other places of worship. People gave up food and stopped shaving for days at a time in return for their prayers to save Mr. Bachchan. The sense of heaviness in the national mood lingered for days until Amitabh Bachchan was declared out of danger. There were traditional prayer vigils, called *Jaagran,* held on streets. The Prime Minister Mrs. Indira Gandhi, at the time was on a trip to the United Kingdom. Instead of returning to New Delhi, the national capital, she went straight to Mumbai, where Amitabh Bachchan was being treated. To this day, after more than thirty years, he is still considered the king of Indian cinema and called the 'Big B' of Bollywood. He also hosts the famous TV quiz show, part of the world's richest franchise of *Who Wants To Be A Millionaire?* If you want to start a conversation with an Indian vendor, ask about the Big B's latest movie; I am sure you will end up being the best-served customer.

So what is 'Bollywood'? Until 1996, Mumbai was called Bombay and it was the epicenter of Indian cinematic activity, as Hollywood is in the United States, so the popular media started to call Indian cinema 'Bollywood'. As a country, India releases more than a thousand movies a year, more than half of which are credited to Bollywood. By a rough calculation, that is more than three movies a day for Indians to digest. These numbers are astonishing, and sometimes I wonder if some countries produce fewer home videos.

There are some actors and actresses who have a shrine dedicated to them by their enthusiastic fans. When the actor-politician MGR from a southern state of India died, twenty-one fans committed suicide. Since twenty-one is an auspicious number among Hindus, those enthusiastic fans sacrificed themselves to try to restore MGR's life on earth.

India is a very conservative and traditional society. Age plays a very important part in relationships between man and a woman. Romantic lovers are assumed to be of nearly the same age with an acceptable societal tolerance of four or five years. If the difference is greater, the relationship tends to be considered similar to that of an elder brother or father. But for actor Rajinikant, this restriction is never enforced. He has worked in romantic roles with actresses half his age. Together they have danced like teenagers and fans have not only appreciated but admired him too. Of course, as always, the makeup artists and digital editors have a challenging task at hand as Rajnikant keeps growing in age as well as popularity. Imagine Jack Nicholson of today starring in John Travolta role in *Grease*, along with those teenagers. Even more astonishing is the record-breaking box-office returns that Rajnikant's movies generate.

It is very easy to understand Indian movies. They over-explain each intricacy in the plot in order to educate audiences of all intelligence. No one must be left behind, seems to be the motto. The characters are shown thinking aloud so we hear their secret planning. Hence, the concept of movies in India are still struggling to metamorphose itself from school plays and evolving into cinema with intelligent plots.

There are a few blockbuster movies which have been continuously running successfully in a particular theater for more than fifteen years. People are never tired of watching them. I have met a few Indians who have watched a particular movie for more than twenty-five times. People memorize the dialogue of those iconic movies and consider it as a status symbol of some sort. Many a party games, for both adults and children, involve reciting dialogue from blockbuster movies. When Obama wanted to connect with Indians, he too had to recite lines from Bollywood.

I will not mention the role of songs at parties, as description of Bollywood songs may warrant a separate book of its own!

For those watching an Indian movie, it will be astonishing how the movies have songs and dances intertwined, as in music videos. After every fifteen minutes in the plot, a music video threads the story with an emotion, and may even take the story forward dramatically. These are songs which Indians hum and sing at parties and in bathrooms alike. People are so charmed by the music and the lyrics of these songs that they are memorized by hundreds. Ask any Indian and they will be able to sing or hum at least a hundred songs even when unconscious.

In fact, there is a party game called *Antakshari*, not found elsewhere in the world. Here the participants have to sing a song starting with the letter of the alphabet which ended the previous song. Believe me; this game can go on for a whole night and even longer. People have a huge memory database for these Indian movie songs. The amazing thing about this game is that it attracts participation from all ages and sexes. I would be surprised if any marriage party, birthday, or other social gathering in India would be complete without this game being played.

In one instance, the audiences in the cinema were so enthralled by a particular song that they actually stopped the film midway, until the projectionist repeated the song several times. By now, one would have realized that India is really a nation of moviegoers and those movies are deeply engrained in the national psyche. If you are still wondering what Bollywood movies are like, just imagine all movies are similar to the famous Hollywood musicals *Mamma Mia* or *Moulin Rouge!*

The audiences for Indian movies are mixed. There is hardly any strict market segment that could define the audience. A choice of genre is too far-fetched an idea, hence the directors mix all the genres and typical plots such as thriller, romance, car chases, family drama, personal sacrifices, gun battles, all punctuated with songs and dances. Everyone must leave the theater happy. These movies are called 'Masala' movies, or a grand mixture of spiced-up emotions.

Usually the movies are made to run for three hours, with an intermission of ten to fifteen minutes. If you are watching an Indian movie, brace yourself for that 180-minute ride on an emotional roller coaster. The bright side of Indian movies is that they are predictable, down to the moment when you should expect a song or dance sequence.

Indian cinema directors and producers are not only creative in making movies; they are also creative in borrowing pieces of plots, scenes, locations and music from the Hollywood movies. It is not termed as copyright infringement, but thought of as 'inspiration'. So there are hundreds of songs, plots or even entire movies inspired by the west. They include Hollywood blockbuster movies like *The Bodyguard, Where Eagles Dare, Ghost, Seven Brides for Seven Brothers* and many others.

Unlike music videos, where the player on the stage is also the actual singer, in Bollywood, the face on the screen is not the actual singer, but instead is lip-synching with a playback singer. The playback singers are highly talented and the pinnacle of experts in vocal music. They are often more popular than the actors on the screen. The singer called "The Nightingale of India", Lata Mangeshkar, has been a playback artist for more than seventy years and has sung more than 50,000 songs in thirty-six different languages. Even the Guinness Book of Records has lost count of her songs and movies, I mean almost. They do not post records any more. It is a feat in itself and a world record to be admired for many more generations to come.

Historically, the role of movies and cinema is not limited to mere entertainment. The elderly in India tell me, in the arranged marriage system, the boy's and girl's families used to meet each other at a particular cinema or at the temple before deciding to formalize the relationship. The families on both sides would decide on a movie show, where an informal meeting with the prospective spouse was arranged. Like the movie, if the families got on well, the next step was decided; otherwise they just had some more tunes to hum and songs to sing.

Finally, if you lose your way through the maze of Indian roads, there is a good chance that you will be directed via a cinema theater as your landmark. It is very common to find the name of a cinema theater in a postal address, directing the postman to 'opposite', 'behind', 'next to', or even just 'near to'!

Bollywood is omnipotent. Its influence is so strong and meshed into the Indian mental fabric that readers will find references in most of the chapters of this book. It would be to either indicate where Bollywood has changed Indian thinking or how Indian Bollywood metamorphosed itself. I think the remaining chapters would remain incomplete in their essence, if Bollywood remained unmentioned.

90% of Indian movies are predictable. Here is a list of predictable parts of the plot:

- The Indian police will always arrive very late, so late that their presence in the plot is redundant.

- The villain is always very rich.

- The hero, though he appears to be slim and weak, can handle a dozen experts in martial arts.

- The firearm always jams out at the last moment.

- The hero has to give out a long sermon, which remains incomplete though, before shooting the villain.

- Other than Indian police, all other country's police are stupid and can be fooled.

- Either the hero is filthy rich, owns luxury cars, private jets and mansions, or he lives in poverty with a terminally ill mother.

- When it comes to bravery and solving his problems like heartbreak and a villain's atrocity, a teetotaler hero takes the support of alcohol.

- There are no Indian movies which leave a bar intact after a gun battle. All the players with their shooting equipment miss targets, only to sacrifice yet another bottle of expensive spirits.

- The doctor makes a home visit with an official bag and a stethoscope. The doctor uses this stethoscope to provide an expert opinion about very critical ailments like cancer. He is also able to predict the time left for the terminally ill patients.
  - There are more than six bullets in a revolver for the hero.

- The hero never misses a gunshot and so does his beautiful and delicate heroine.

- If a boy and a girl get drenched in rain or beach, they will have sex with a Bollywood song number and pregnancy is sure to follow.

- If the villain is a smuggler, he will have a propeller driven four seated aircraft, which will fail to take-off at the last moment.

- If the hero plays the cop, he is always in the rank of 'Police Inspector'.

2nd C - Cricket

Nothing can beat cricket fever in any sporting season. The happiness of the nation can be measured by the performance of the Indian cricket team. There might be some discussion and analysis about the composition of the team or player's inclusion, but most Indians are just interested in whether the Indian team wins or not.

You must see the streets when India plays their arch-rival Pakistan. It is as if two countries have gone to war AGAIN. The roads are deserted and malls are like ghost towns. People settle down in front of their televisions and all other appointments are put on hold. If you are flying between cities, the pilots are usually courteous enough to give passengers an update on the latest score. At the traffic lights, usually the guy on a two wheeler will ask the four wheeler driver to share the latest score, which he readily obliges in a unique gesture of national bonding.

Though cricket is played by very few countries in the world, mainly by erstwhile British colonies, the significant numbers of the population who are thrilled by every stroke in the game, make it one of the most watched sports apart from the Olympics.

Like all major sporting world cups and the Olympics, the Cricket World Cup also moves around the globe to different host countries. Every time the Indian team participates, right from the build-up till the end, cricket becomes the national topic of conversation. The entire nation comes together. People go to temples and mosques to pray for India to beat the world. There are special prayer services conducted across cities. The towns where particular members of the cricket team live become the center of attention, especially their own houses and neighborhoods.

Bollywood artists are not left behind in showing their commitment to the Indian World Cup team. They release songs and cheer on the players like soldiers marching to war, making patriotism the sole reason for playing cricket. On all red carpets Bollywood events, happening around the time of Cricket World Cup, the journalists would ask Film Stars about India's winning chances, do they think the selection of team is appropriate, or whether such player will be able to perform. Some film stars are not very keen cricket fans; still they have to answer those questions in order to improve their fan following. Only twice in recent years India has reached the finals. The atmosphere became so charged up with emotion that you could almost imagine the earth might start revolving faster.

Whenever India wins a major tournament, as they did in 2011, where they won the World Cup, the celebrations are unrestrained. The excitement went on for weeks and all the state governments (twenty-nine in number) played host to the winning team. No expense was spared. Parades around the towns and cities become a daily occurrence.

If the team arrives from abroad after winning the World Cup, the roads to the airport are unlikely to be clear that day. Like the weather, it is wise to check the Indian cricket team's tournament schedule before traveling to India.

As you might imagine, being a cricketer in India is like living in seventh heaven. TV shows, talks, interviews, press, advertising, product endorsements and public appearances flood a cricketer's schedule. But it lasts only until the next performance, which could be within weeks.

Indians are poor team players, except when they play cricket.

Then there is the other side to this craze. Indians think it is their duty to pray and motivate their players with fanatical verbal support, and therefore the players must win the tournament. There is no excuse for not winning the World Cup, so if India performs poorly, the players' homes are stoned and vandalized. There could be threats to the players and security is increased to restore calm. The players are booed and could receive a very cold reception for months to come. The captain might even have to quit.

The extreme popularity of cricket has made other sports less popular and therefore, their sportsmen and women are financially very poor. One can say that there exists only one sport in India, which like many other significant legacies is also an important reminiscence of British Empire.

Usually, Indians are very poor team players because they have an inherent selfish habit of keeping things to themselves, especially if it gives them public attention. Perhaps their poverty has made them inherently possessive. But cricket defies this national characteristic of individualism. This is the one team sport that has brought success and glory to the nation. Some of the cricketers are compared to God, which clearly means much more than being a poster boy. In short, Cricket is unofficial religion of Indians.

In the days when the radio commentary was the primary source of cricketing information, I know stories of fans that have stayed home from work and kept note of the score sheets for all the cricket matches that India played. As a result, they also risked their careers to listen to the radio commentary. If you were able to quote statistics of a particular match, it was nothing short of being a local celebrity. It is different now though, in the age of mobiles & multimedia.

No other sport holds the position of a national activity as cricket does in India. You can find Indians of all ages playing cricket in narrow alleys (called 'Gulley'), in parks, on beaches and even in the corridors of apartment buildings. A cricket bat and balls are a necessary part of a picnic kit. In fact, cricket played in the alleys, called 'gulley' cricket, is so famous that one of the Indian female model-turned- commentator took to making a famous television series about it. She toured the length and breadth of the country, playing and filming 'gulley' cricket with people of all ages. Although, secretly people tell me they loved her spaghetti-strap blouses and exotic *sarees* (the native Indian dress) more than her cricketing expertise. I think it was just that perfect mix of the fundamentals of Indian society, the cricket and glamour that made her a television personality.

3rd C – Congress

Politically, India is a very active country. If the news headlines do not mention political news, then something is considered wrong with the report. With these national expectations, it is important to be aware of who's who in Indian politics.

Indian National Congress, or 'Congress' in general parlance was the political party at the forefront of the Indian independence movement and has been at the helm of affairs to date. The party has been prominent for 129 years in the history of India. It has also produced the most celebrated politicians, including Mahatma Gandhi. Unsurprisingly, Indians tend to look towards this party, for either its actions or inaction.

A background to the Congress party is an essential for anyone dealing with Indians. India was a British colony up to 1947. The struggle for freedom from the British Empire lasted nearly a hundred years, and, for nearly fifty-five years of that time, Congress as a party was engaged in that struggle. So for the greater part of the freedom struggle, Congress was synonymous with independence from British rule. The stalwarts of the Indian freedom struggle were mostly members of the Congress party, so the popular appeal of the Congress continued with the free and independent India.

Statistically, of sixty-seven years of Indian independence, nearly fifty years have been under Congress rule in central government. In this sense, the Congress party has been regarded by many as akin to a monarchy of the country. The effect of this pseudo-monarchy has led to India being governed by at least some members of the Nehru-Gandhi family, even to this day. So it is a joint monarchy between Congress and the Nehru-Gandhi family. Also, until 1990, there was no political alternative in India, either to Congress or to the Nehru-Gandhi family. In 67 years of Indian independence, the Nehru-Gandhi family has been at the helm of affairs for over sixty years. Although this has not been designed that way, in political circles the fact remains that Congress and the Nehru-Gandhi dynasty are inseparably part of the Indian psyche. It is like the everlasting royal charter for the House of Windsor in the United Kingdom. Wherever, whenever there is political activity in India, be that in student unions, on village councils, in municipalities, state or central governments, Congress is represented on the podium. Although it would be incorrect to say that Congress is the only political party in India, it would be absolutely correct to say that all other parties devise their policies with reference to the Congress. Though the political landscape in India has changed drastically in 2014, there is still a special place for the Congress party in Indian politics.

When talking to Indians about politics, on which all Indians think they are experts, it is important to judge whether the mention of Congress will help your discussion or not. It is also important to note that Indians follow a particular political party for their whole life. This could also be handed down from previous generations. This usually happens with followers of the right-wing Hindu nationalist party, the BJP, and the communist party. In a discussion, it is advisable to wait until the traffic lights are clearly visible or you could end up on the wrong side, forever.

By now, you will have an idea of how clearly Indian society is demarcated when it comes to taking sides. For someone new to the company of Indians, taking sides is mandatory in order to win loyalty. At some point in time during a discussion, sooner or later an Indian will discuss local, national or international politics. It forms a major chunk of their attitudes and perspective.

4th C – Corruption

Even in India, 'corruption' is a dirty word, as in all other countries, although it has a peculiar place in Indian society. Let us say, it is a scapegoat on which all the ills of Indian society can be blamed. If the roads are bad, blame it on corruption; delayed flights, foul-smelling railway coaches, accidents, poor health services, etc. can be easily attributed to corruption, even without investigating the real reason. Even if you were to investigate, the search would almost certainly stop at someone who had been corrupt. Human error or machine failure are not even a consideration. It is understood that if palms are greased well, everything runs smoothly with surprising efficiency. Because it is a way of life, by natural instinct Indians are able to make an accurate guess about the corruption involved in a particular malfunctioning system.

So what is this corruption? Any instance where the intended funds from the government coffers are diverted into personal pockets is classified as corruption. There could be an encyclopedia written about corrupt practices in India. Many of those who do not have access to public money though, still in public jobs, indulge in the act of bribery. In the west, we cannot imagine openly paying airport customs officers to allow illegal imports, or paying a traffic officer to ignore a violation, but it is a way of life in India. Any law can be bypassed using the practice of bribery, or as it is understood, paying money 'under the table'. It is so prevalent that it is no longer a case of any violation, but instead it has become 'speed money', with the assurance of getting things done fast.

The work could be a small job like the installation of a landline phone, getting a passport, a driver's license or clearances for property. The big ones include multi-billion dollars' worth of national assets stolen from government coffers. Many are reported as scams in the media. The scams reported are so numerous that at one time it was very common to expect a scam a day. People are so tired of talking about scams that they now post a list on social media to keep a track.

The funniest of the scams is the 'fodder scam'. It breaks records for being perpetrated by the silliest scammer trying to fool the country in plain sight. The chief of a state was involved in selling fodder for cattle which did not exist, transporting the fodder for those fictitious thousands of cattle for thousands of kilometers, on a vehicle registered as a two-wheeler. If there was a section in the *Guinness World Records* for ridiculous scams, this Indian entry would be the winner.

You can openly talk about 'speed money' or even negotiate the rate if the work requires bulk services. It is no longer a taboo. The national fabric has been woven with this 'money under the table'. On the bright side, I would say 'grease money' can beat the most efficient systems across the world when it comes to getting things done.

Although there have been changes in governments because of corruption scandals, people, the press and the larger population in general are still involved in it. After living in India for so long, I would say it is not possible for a common Indian to be corruption-free. If you do not give bribes, you are probably stuck at an important stage, forever. I am not marketing this practice as an efficiency tool, but letting readers know, in preparation for dealing with things in India.

Here is a definitive case that you will never miss in India. Indian railways are huge. At any point in time, some 14,000 trains are running over 75,000 kilometers of track. There are some twenty million Indians riding on these trains as you read this sentence. But catering to the national travel plans for a population of 1.2 billion Indians is a mammoth task. I would say it is almost a superhuman task to provide reservations for journey. By now you will have guessed where the fun of bribery starts.

The ticket collector, called the TTE or TC, identified as the person in the black jacket on the train, is the key person. Unfortunately, if you are without a confirmed reservation, due to last-minute travel plans or a busy holiday season, then approaching the TTE is what most people do. They approach only when he is not surrounded by other passengers hovering around him, for the same reason as yours. Sometimes during the season, the bribe to get a berth on the train can be as much as three to four times the price of the ticket itself. It is a common practice, and the going rate for a railway reservation ticket for a particular season can be openly discussed.

There are further details about the lifestyle on Indian railways in a separate chapter.

Corruption in India is a fascinating discussion topic and probably one of the most popular. Particularly interesting, is gossip about the incredibly high value of some scams that have been reported. They can easily range from one billion dollars to fifty billion dollars. This may seem unbelievable, but it is a reality of life in India.

People traveling to India will see the consequences of corruption in the infrastructure, dealings and discussions. The heightened level of frustration is visible, and you might be saddened too.

Indians are delighted to visit developed nations and willing to stay abroad. They would also draw endless comparisons with what would have been possible in India. Equally significant will be the narratives that fellow Indians will receive once they are back in India.

5th C - Caste system

India is a Teflon-hard, hierarchical society. Everyone has their position in the layers that define this society of 1.2 billion people. Caste and religion are embossed in an individual's name, surname, festivals they celebrate, rituals they follow, the conduct of marriages and business transactions. Even finding love happens within the caste system. There have been great fights, discussions and political upheaval against the caste system in India, yet everyone still loves their caste. If the caste system were limited to classification within an equal society, it would work wonders. But caste defines each citizen in layers of superiority and inferiority.

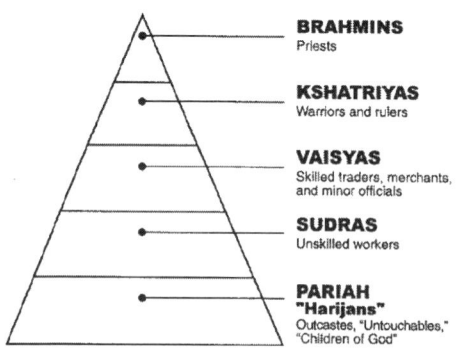

BRAHMINS
Priests

KSHATRIYAS
Warriors and rulers

VAISYAS
Skilled traders, merchants, and minor officials

SUDRAS
Unskilled workers

PARIAH
"Harijans"
Outcastes, "Untouchables,"
"Children of God"

How is a caste defined? It is by being born into a family, or in simplistic terms, by inheritance. So, one is really screwed, right from birth. It defines the surname to be used, whom to marry, which traditions to follow and even which Gods to worship. In rural India, the caste will define the body language of a person, the place to sit within a group, the dignity one will receive in society and even the location of one's house in the village. It also defines the kind of guest that can come over. In a way, caste defines the national fabric in an informal way, but strictly coded.

Someone born into the upper caste has to worry less, with reference to the general treatment in society. In rural India, members of the upper caste automatically dominate others. The caste defines where a religious festival will be held, or which well (water source) can be used to draw water by the lower caste. If you are born into a lower caste, however rich one may become, you need to be prepared to be mistreated. The upper caste has license to be treated as superior, even if they are incapable.

The Indian caste system gets the credit for outsmarting even those religions which initially did not have stratifications. The Muslims, Christians, Sikhs, Jains and Buddhists living in India have been sliced and diced too. According to Wikipedia, there are four major castes, 3,000 sub-castes and more than 90,000 indigenous sub-groups. Indians also have a state identity like being Kashmiri, Punjabi, Gujarati, Rajasthani, Bihari, Bengali, Tamilian, Telugu, Marathi, Oriya and other identities of the twenty-nine states of India. I have found that Indians do not easily gel with people from other states. Even if the city or town is cosmopolitan, still an employee affinity, recruitment and business preferences are with others from one's own state or caste.

As India is clearly divided by its ethnic identities, so is the common behavior of Indians. Indians try to find someone from their state whenever they are among strangers or in a new environment. This leads to actively making cliques in offices, corporate boardrooms, sports teams, neighborhoods, schools and even with maids, drivers and cleaners. Surprisingly, Indians also run temples, educational institutions and charitable organizations on ethnic lines.

For foreign companies recruiting Indians to work abroad, the caste system is not very prevalent until the time it reaches a critical mass. Once the regions are appropriately represented, they do start to form a miniature India, with all the relevant slicing and dicing. The US is home to the Telugu Association of North America, and the London Tamil Sangam (Confluence) resides in the UK. The Maharastra Mondal London and the Bihar Association of Canada carry the spirit of their respective states outside India, which suggests that being Indian is not just a nationality, but more a composition of statehood, religion and caste.

Cleaning our Homes

Unlike western countries, where carpets are a requirement, Indian houses have hard floors of ceramic tiles, concrete or stones. Hence the cleaning habits are different. They require a two-step cleaning method. The first step is sweeping the loose dust off the floor and collecting it in one corner. You might not believe how much dust there is. The achievement is when the cleaner collects that dust from all corners of the house, with a sense of pride. If there is not enough dust collected, then it is considered not to be done properly. The amount of dust collected is necessary for the assessment of effective sweeping. The next round is mopping with a wet cloth. Every household must do this process daily and in some households it might be done twice a day. The concept of vacuum cleaning is not prevalent in India, although some Indians buy one as a status symbol. Wall-to-wall carpet is for the rich or five-star hotels.

The first thing Indians notice when travelling abroad is the extensive carpeting that buildings have in the west.

In southern Indian cities, the place in front of the gates is washed every morning and decorated with colorful patterns on the floor. It is called *Rangoli*. In the eastern states, the houses are smoke-filled in the evening to ward off evil or any germs in the air.

Sunlight is a must. The curtains are not drawn, especially in the morning. It is considered that morning sunshine brings good luck and purity to the house. In effect, the Indians are obsessive about cleaning their homes.

In rural India and in many urban homes too, the dishes are cleaned with ashes and mud. Dishwashers are not prevalent at all, as a continuous water supply from taps is still not a reality.

The Indians keep their houses clean, but their surroundings filthy. It is a common site for residents to throw in the garbage in a public place which could be a few feet away from their home.

Cycles are for the poor

India may be the largest manufacturer of bicycles in the world, after China, yet there are no ace cyclists competing in the Olympics. Cycles are for poor. They are just inexpensive conveyances to get to places. Little do Indians realize that people in the west often bike for pleasure. It would sound unusual to an Indian, if you shared your cycling experiences. For most Indians, leisure using transportation means nothing. While driving is a necessity, flying is a luxury.

Bicycles are mostly black in color with just one speed gear. Brakes are levered rather than the wired ones found in the west. Cyclists in India are brave as they are not required to wear helmets. If you do wear a helmet, you might look as if you are over-protecting yourself. The view of the bicycle as a poor man's vehicle is so ingrained in the Indian mindset that an Indian living abroad would not bike either to work or for leisure. So now you know that suggesting a walk or a drive is a better option for Indians.

Cycle repair shops are plentiful along the road side. They also repair flat tires and top up pressure using hand pumps. Bikes are also a poor man's family transportation, where the children sit on the front bar and the wife is on the pillion. Indian innovation has come up with a child seat on the handlebars, for the convenience of young and tender bones.

How can you figure out if the female on the bicycle is his girlfriend or wife? According to Bollywood movies, romantic scenes are portrayed with the girl, nearly cheek to cheek, sitting side-saddle on the front bar of the cycle. Wives are less privileged, as they are always riding pillion, carrying the baby. In India, during last twenty-five years, nothing much has changed in terms of expressing love on the bicycle. Instead, they are now replaced by 125 cc motorcycles with fancy names to show their great engineering and power. The entire family rides the bike, with the children squeezed between the man and the wife. A wife, as always, rides pillion, sitting sidesaddle and probably holding another infant. If the lady on the pillion is sitting astride, there is a high probability that she is not married to the man riding the bike.

The most useful part of the Indian bicycle is the carrier, which has to be sturdy enough to double as a carrier for a human load and for business goods. Indian milkmen traditionally hang large fifty liter cans on either side. When delivering milk, they ride up to the address, park their bicycles, reach their measuring jar into the milk and pour it into the customer's container. It is that simple. 99% of the country's milk is delivered with this methodology, using either a bicycle or a motorcycle. So also is the gossips about the neighborhood and I am pretty sure it is not going to change in the next fifty years.

Corporate Indians – Grownup Kids

Schools strongly influence corporations. It is not wrong to say that corporations are like schools, only that there are grownups. All the habits of the school are followed through to the workplace. The bosses are highly respected. They are never questioned and at times files and papers may be thrown at employees by the bosses without any objection.

Working hours, like those school homework hours, are long and tedious.

If school children are teacher pleasers, working Indians are Boss pleasers.

Working with Indians in a corporation will give you a few questions to be answered. Everything has to be a "Yes". Like being a teacher-pleaser at school, all Indians are people-pleasers. Hence, they rarely say "No" for an answer, even if they know the 'impossibility' of the task.

Firstly, it is considered rude, secondly, it hurts one's superiority, thirdly, accepting "No" will set a wrong precedent of being a weak leader and the superior's superior will be annoyed about being too flexible and giving things away easily. Easily yielding to an employee's request is a taboo. I know cases where employees have changed their dates for a marriage, engagement or a family vacation in order to accommodate a routine requirement by the employer.

As in schools, Indians do not want to sound stupid by seeking clarification. Even though their work might go in the wrong direction and will require rework, this is still fine with them. Coming in time to the office and leaving late makes an Indian, sincere. At least that is the impression it creates in the organization. Certainly, strictly sticking to the office hours, will make things worse. The smartness of the employee is after office hours. As a job description is not tightly defined, superiors can give as much work as possible and employee has to take that much in order to grow. The lure of growing and the peer competition makes an Indian work harder than their contemporaries in the west.

> **INDIAN WORK LIFE BALANCE :**
> **Work comes first,**
> **life is after re-birth,**
> **and**
> **God holds the balance to judge.**

Like the classrooms in the school, where the class is packed with sixty children, offices are also packed with employees. Per capita space to work is much less than compared to the US or European standards. Many times, the phone numbers and instruments are shared which means that your colleague will be talking over your shoulder while works requires focus and concentration. Whether the furniture matches the best practices of ergonomics, is absolutely out of the question.

Along with the company secrets, stationary is also a guarded secret. Companies keep an official register, manned by a full time staff to issue and log the stationary consumption. Why do the companies do that, is a puzzle. Certainly this practice puts them into the category of being 'pound foolish'?

We all know India is a hub of call centers and we are no longer surprised if most of our calls are answered by an Indian with an English name. Behind the scenes, these call centers run like a typical Indian school, where discipline is enforced with an iron fist. A lunch break can be metered in minutes; tea, toilet and tobacco breaks could be just fifteen or twenty minutes in an eight-hour shift. Any deviation from this discipline can get you fired from a job because there are a dozen others in a queue, waiting for this position. Every day is like an exam, not only for the employees, but for the employers too, because the Philippines, Brazil, Egypt and others are serious competition to the Indian call centers.

Even though the agents might sound polite and courteous to you, except for the odd one, the background is in stark contrast. Imagine that while they are talking to you, breathing over these agents' shoulders are their demon-like managers, wielding swords in one hand and dangling a stopwatch in another. It is a miracle and a human achievement in itself to survive in a job like this. I suspect even the angels working from the comfort of heaven would not keep their cool and stay polite if they were working in those call centers.

D

- Date of Birth – Many
- Driving in India
- Drinking Means Drunk

Date of Birth - Many

Very few nationalities can boast of having multiple dates of birth in one life. Until recently in India, there was no formal recordkeeping of hospital births. Many parents wouldn't ask for an official birth certificate, or may lose it in the piles of old daily newspapers (*Raddi*). Also, these parents followed the Hindu calendar to record the child's birth, which is the lunar calendar and drastically different from the English calendar. Therefore, at birth itself, an Indian has at least two dates of birth, one from the Hindu calendar and the other according to the Christian calendar.

Most Indians born earlier than the 1980s had their date of birth recorded by their school. Parents would not like to keep their child at home for an extra year, if the child was young by a few months to join a new school session. They intentionally declared a false date of birth, which would allow their child to start school earlier. By the time a child is at school, he might have three 'official' dates of birth.

Having a flexible Indian age is an advantage for Indian parents when traveling. The reduction on a half ticket makes a flexible age handiest. Often you find parents arguing with the railway authorities about the age of a child, because the mother is carrying an extra grown-up child in her arms to avoid paying for her 'baby'. The parents argue with pride about their healthy baby, while the railway man questions the age of the child.

Indian children continue to dodge the bus and railway authorities to secure age reductions, so a child could have an age spanning from seven to eleven. In a nutshell, an Indian child could actually be aged ten, eleven according to school records, eight while traveling on a bus, seven for the railways, and of course eighteen as a Facebook® user.

Multiple dates of birth are also used conveniently in arranging marriage to find the right kind of groom and bride. The age difference between the boy and the girl plays a significant role in the arranged marriage system. It is the first criterion for match making. The girl must be younger than the boy, from a few months up to 7-8 years. In some cases, where the girl's parents realize that age is the only barrier, there is a good chance of using the trump card of flexible age. The boy's family might never come to know about this age manipulation.

Many readers will not believe this. Recently, the chief of the Indian army dragged the government of India into court for considering the wrong date of birth to retire him from the services. Although it was assumed to be more of a clerical error between the date of birth recorded in the army school and the date used by the HR department, the discrepancy survived for forty years of the general's career. As with many wonders of the world, multiple dates of birth for millions of Indians, unlike anywhere else on earth, can lead the world's second largest army into a fight with its own government.

Having multiple dates of birth is no secret, so often people check with each other about which specific birth date they are using.

Driving in India

Someone who has driven in India can drive anywhere else in the world. This saying is common among those who have experience of driving in other countries. Rough terrain is only one part of the driving experience. Add to that, the unpredictability of variables provided by living beings, becomes a unique challenge.

All Indian pedestrians are called 'HERO'.

A few examples might include situations such as a pedestrian appearing from nowhere, jumping aside if you honk. The driver usually races faster to cross the pedestrian, and so also tries the pedestrian. No Indian wants to slow down or stop for a petty reason like letting someone else go first. If for some reason, the pedestrian does come in front of the four-wheeler, along with a honk, the shouting driver calls him as 'Hero' and strongly advises him to move aside.

Drivers rarely stop or slow down for the fire brigade or an ambulance, though they do for the police, because the consequences of not doing so can be really nasty.

Keeping in the right lane is not possible. There are many reasons to it. To start, there are no clearly-marked lanes. Either the contractor did a slapdash job with the paint, or the heavy traffic has worn away the road markings. Secondly, the road is full of vehicles of all shapes and sizes, from hand-pulled carts to two-wheelers, three-wheelers and many-wheelers. The intervening space is packed with pedestrians and vendors. Thirdly, Indians believe in having a relaxed relationship with their surroundings, including traffic rules. So why bother? Fourthly, on the street, Indians park their vehicle as close as possible to their destination. Therefore, obstacles are everywhere on the road. Finally, zebra crossings are just there for bureaucracy. The width of the crossing cannot handle the smallest fraction of the pedestrians that cross the street. People try to take the shortest route between destinations across the road which may be few hundred meters away from the Zebra crossing.

A classic case is where the vehicle ahead applies its brakes suddenly, to pick up a waving passenger. Animals such as cows, dogs and buffalo are common on the streets and on highways. The drivers have to do their best to anticipate their random movement. Side indicators are rarely used, so drivers tend to use hand signals. Litter from the vehicle ahead of you might fly out all over the place, and of course there is a risk of flying spit from a passing bus. Vehicles jumping red lights during the night are very common, and speeding by drunk drivers is nothing new.

Honk as much as you like, to stay safe.

There are some habits that help mitigate these risks and should be adopted by one and all on the roads of India. Honk as much as you like. Let the journey be punctuated with the sound of the horn, so that those in danger can move away. This will also help on the streets and highways that are one-way. Since it is the vehicle's visibility that keeps away danger on the road, Indians drive with their headlights on full beam at night. There is no better way to see that danger is approaching. Those who are aware that life is precious will automatically make way.

Seat belts are mandatory for manufacturers to provide, but unfortunately not for passengers to wear. For Indians it is an inconvenience, and even the Prime Minister will often be seen not wearing one. If one is caught by law enforcement personnel, Indians prefer to get away by paying a bribe or by dropping a few big names. There are still millions of vehicles traveling on Indian roads which don't have seat belts at all. Why should this be a surprise?

At traffic signals, vehicles queuing at a red light start to honk, even before the signal turns green. In metropolitan cities, there could be some hundred vehicles waiting impatiently to cross a junction with a traffic signal. When the image of an angry Indian boss haunts the poor Indians being late, then honking to release their impatience is the only way out, whether the signal has turned green or not. Traffic signals are also a hot spot for transacting business. Since the stoppage lasts more than a couple of minutes, there will be vendors knocking on the windows to sell bottled water, magazines, best seller books, newspapers, flower bouquets, laundry bags, incense sticks, exotic fruits like strawberries, superstitious and religious materials and even window cleaning services. If this supermarket at the traffic lights is not enough, eunuchs also pass by seeking tips for their blessings and expressing their wrath with severe curses if someone fails to offer one. Traffic signals are a hot-spot for begging.

Vehicles bellowing thick clouds of black smoke are not a rare occurrence, which makes the shirt collar dirty within first half of the day itself. It is possible that the exhaust of the truck standing close to you at a red signal might puff out smoke releasing hydrocarbons horizontally into another vehicle with open windows, or choking the rider of a two-wheeler on a hot summer morning. Call it pollution or just a way of life, millions of two-wheeler commuters negotiate this situation daily on their way to work.

For an Indian, the driver ahead is always too slow, so people either honk to make him go faster or irritate him to give way. If neither works, it is still possible to overtake from any side where space allows. Oncoming traffic has to manage the maneuver or simply come to a head-on collision. On average, a hundred thousand people lose their lives every year to the drama played out on Indian roads.

Driving at night is even more perilous, if the day time adventures were not enough. The oncoming traffic can have vehicles which do not have both headlights working properly. There is a high possibility that neither works. So, what does an Indian do? They all drive by frequently alternating between low and high beam. This innovation also helps them avoid colliding from the rear with a vehicle that is parked in the dark.

Like Indian movies, driving on Indian roads is also entertaining. The trucks and three-wheeled auto rickshaws are painted in vibrant colors, with images of Bollywood stars, Gods and Goddesses, sacred animals and plenty of philosophical scriptures. It is a delight to see these paintings and read those homegrown and unique practical tips, freely displayed. These works of art are now being recognized as 'Indian Truck Art' and there are umpteen scholars finding interest in documenting what goes on behind the scenes of these street masterpieces. Usually they are in native languages, sometimes in English too, but the exciting part is the misspelled words and odd phrases in English that make these scriptures adorable. A few translated examples are 'Guests are God', 'Driving thrills, Drinking Kills', 'Don't fall for the curves', 'Mother's Blessing to all', 'Take poison, but do not believe girls', 'Insult to all those who are jealous', 'Bachelor Staff', 'We two and our two' and last but not least 'Drive Safe—someone is waiting'.

Drinking Means Drunk

While it is a part of some cultures to consume wine and spirits on every occasion, India views drinking in its own way. There is no dividing line between drinking and getting drunk. The general impression of people drinking alcohol is very poor. They are considered loose in character and not dependable for any serious responsibilities, even when they are not under the influence of alcohol. This typecasting is not imaginary, but based on years of what society has witnessed.

Those who drink alcohol do not just drink, rather they consume it constantly. Often they are seen swaying on the streets, intoxicated and annoying people. Their families at some point in time have to bear financial hardship and domestic violence due to addiction. Those who have had fame and wealth have also misbehaved in public under the influence of alcohol. They have bullied people to whatever extent their powers allowed them. Many high-profile hit-and-run cases have involved well-known personalities driving under the influence of alcohol. This has only added to the poor record and the growing conviction that drinking is a source of social ills.

Along with the law, Indian society is also lenient with those who get drunk. Many give the excuse of being out of their senses while misbehaving. No wonder that in India, drinking means getting drunk.

Alcohol also means Alcoholics.

Unlike in the west, the shops in India, which sell alcohol, are the most protected and the least fancy places in the entire market. Like the iron bars that restrict prisoners in jail, most shops operate from behind bars. Customers have to pay first before the salesman brings the product, or else there is a good chance that customers would never pay and just run away.

Womenfolk dare not go near these shops. There is a high probability that someone drunk might either verbally or physically abuse them.

How can Bollywood be left behind in stereotyping the image of drinking? Baring few, nearly all Indian movies show villains drinking, having meetings in and around a lavish home bar. They are also shown partying, with skimpy clad girls performing, while serving alcohol. In contrast, the good guy is always a teetotaler and if found at a party with the villains, looks lost and amazed.

E

- Exit – Missing the Knowhow
- Eating Style

Exit – Missing the Knowhow

The Mahabharat is one of the mythological epics that most Indians have read, heard or viewed as a television series and it has a deep influence on their thinking and practice. There is one incident in those mythologies that can be generally identified with Indians. They are all devoid of an 'exit strategy'. As the mythology goes, *Abhimanyu*, the son of the greatest archer, *Arjun*, did not know the art of exiting the enemy fortification, even though he was an ace warrior like his father.

While he was skilled enough to reach the center of the seven-layered fortification, presumed to be more complex than the modern day Pentagon, he met his Waterloo only during his exit.

Similarly, most Indian practices are without an exit strategy. Let us start with marriage. All marriages in India are made in heaven and can last until heaven's door is knocked by one of the two partners. During their time together, couples can go back and forth through hell, but the option to exit from the marriage does not exist. As a culture, exiting from marriage is not acceptable. Although these days a small urban population does leave an abusive relationship, largely it is not part of the culture. Previous generations have seen huge battles between couples, yet they still live together for a lifetime, from honeymoon until natural separation at death.

Most jobs, other than modern day employment in information technology and call centers, are practically permanent. It may not be that employer has assured the employment, as if written in stone, moreover the employee feels sincere loyalty towards their organization. Unfair and unrealistic pay, a tough holiday calendar, extra working hours and even abusive working conditions do not deter their allegiance to the organization. The exit strategy comes into play only when one retires, or when there is a pressing relocation needed, for example, to care for ailing parents or for children's education. Deciding to leave because the organization offers only a limited opportunity to progress is a step taken only by a few. I know organizations where the top ranks are so entrenched that there is no room for upward movement for the next fifteen years, yet people with the best of skill-sets stay there forever. Similarly, year after year, you will find the same waiters in the same restaurant. It is just the same for nurses and teachers too.

Indians strongly believe that their life is a journey. It will come to an end. The big question is how it will end. Like all other developing countries, life in India can come to an abrupt end for very unobvious reasons. Sometimes it could be as evident as overdosing a diabetic patient with glucose, operating on the left side of brain to remove a tumor that was on the right side, or being hit by a speeding vehicle approaching from the wrong direction. When there is so much uncertainty about lifespan in India, and sometimes when life seems too cheap, still people have no life insurance cover. If they have one, it is not enough to support the surviving family. Although there are tax breaks and incentives to purchase insurance cover, still I have seen families completely at a loss, struggling to live with the insurance provided. Indians believe more in spiritual insurance than in financial security. Although life in India is so uncertain, still there is little provision made for accidental exits from this earth.

Interestingly, exit strategy from an Indian point of view means planning for the end. Usually, Indians are poor at planning, or the wisdom to do it develops only after seventy years of age. Writing a Will document is always postponed for the future. If a person is sensible enough to consider writing one, the others in the family do not allow it. It is seen as a bad omen or too uncomfortable to discuss, therefore a better option is to avoid it as long as possible. Interestingly, the Indian civil courts are packed with lawsuits that could have been avoided with basic Will writing, at the appropriate time.

There was a high-profile family feud in the richest family of India. The father left his business empire with the assumption that his sons would continue to live happily together after him. But the children had intentions of their own. Because there was no Will, family feud followed after his death and the stock went crashing. Since market capitalization was significant, so did the response of Indian stock market. After creating the largest business empire in the country, raising the richest Indian kids and surviving a near-fatal stroke, surprisingly enough, it did not give this successful businessman any idea of a soft exit. All one can say is the story of *Abhimanyu* the archer's son was re-lived by this business tycoon. He knew how to make a business empire yet failed to plan his proper exit.

If you are interacting with Indians, you should know that they also have poor judgment about exiting from the conversation. The longer the conversation, the more personal it gets, even though it might be your first meeting. Silence makes Indians very uncomfortable, and they prefer to talk about anything just to fill the silence.

> **Silence makes Indians very uncomfortable.**
> **They talk to try fill Silence.**

Many a times, I have encountered questions about my salary and sources of income, in the first fifteen minutes of our first meeting. This is not considered wrong. The more personal questions are asked, the friendlier the conversation is considered to be. For people living in the west, it could be uncomfortable to have a discussion about such topics until a relationship is established and mature. In India, there is a blurred boundary between formal, informal and business conversation. Most conversations in India are informal, even if they are part of a business interaction.

Eating Style

All Indians eat with their hands. At best, you might find a spoon to help you with the flowing gravy, but it is rarely used. The use of cutlery in India is proportional to how 'posh' you are. The same is the case with restaurants. As the cutlery pieces' increase on your table, the restaurant becomes more expensive and exclusive.

If the combination of frying, roasting, mincing, and sprinkling dozens of spices make the art of Indian cooking, eating with the fingers by rolling, wrapping, tearing, snowballing, finger shoveling a dozen wet and dry dishes around the plate, is the technique of enjoying that art of Indian cooking. An Indian meal requires you to play with all five senses, gifted by God. Touching with the fingers adds to the pleasure. Now you might wonder why burgers, fries, sandwiches and pizzas are a favorite across the world.

The techniques of eating with the hand vary from the north to the south of India. A general rule in northern India is to use only the fingers and not the palm. Otherwise, it will be looked upon as bad manners. It is not difficult to do, as most of the food served in north India is dry and sticks to the Indian bread *(Roti, Nann or Parantha)*. Indian bread is served fresh and hot and is the center of the meal. The accompaniments are the various curry and side dishes, usually no less than four in number. Although the word 'curry' is used extensively in the west, especially in the UK, the word is not prevalently used in India. Since the British in the colonial days were not clearly able to differentiate the dishes or may had difficulty in pronouncing the name correctly, they provided this generic nomenclature for their convenience. It would be respectful to any Indian chef to differentiate the dish with its name.

The bread is broken or split into pieces using the thumb and index finger of both hands. Then these pieces are dipped or wrapped around the curry dishes to make a sizeable nibble. Fingers will get stained, but can be washed later with lime and hot water. This eating style reminds me to caution the readers to wash their hands before sitting down to enjoy an Indian meal. You never know the extent to which the fingers and palms will have to be utilized.

Never use the left hand to eat or serve food, anywhere in India. It is very insulting. The reason for this can be found in the chapter 'Body Language'.

South India is mostly a rice-eating area and side dishes are much more plentiful than in north India. Whether the dishes are served in separate bowls or directly on the rim of the plate, the gravy starts to flow freely around your plate. One side dish might get mixed with another; the liquid from one can flow underneath another dish. One need not worry about the gravy of one dish, mixing with the other, as ultimately they all end up in the same place.

Here in South India, you are free to use the palm to make a ball with a suitable mix of rice and the dish. It is better to avoid dishes flowing down your elbows, but children can do that for fun.

When you are invited by a North Indian or South Indian host, prepare yourself for tackling the varied textures of food which will be served. In both cases, you will be fed to your maximum eating capacity. If you like a particular dish, the host may also offer to pack it up for you. It will be the greatest compliment you can give to your host.

Many restaurants in South India take pride in serving food on banana leaves. Using forks and knives will definitely poke holes into the 'plate' and drip gravy on the table. It is better to eat with your hands on banana leaves, without being embarrassed about spilling morsels outside the plate. It is an acceptable practice.

At home or in an informal setting, Indian do want to close their meals with a glass of water. They drink half of it and wash their fingers and lips with the other half of it. You are right in asking "where the does the waste water flow?". It is no brainer; the chinaware (mostly of stainless steel) is the casualty of being subjected to both Indian's delicacy and the hand wash. The post meal scene might look ugly, but it is better to turn a blind eye than feel embarrassed.

If the situation prevents washing on the table, Indians will never lose an opportunity to walk up to the nearest sink to swish, gargle and spit jet water a few times with roaring sounds louder than a thundering fly past in an air show. Lucky are those who have an Indian guest finishing their meals in a garden. The spit jet will water the lawn around and nurture the flora with the nutritious left over from the mouth.

F

- Foreign Travel
- Fair Complexion Attracts

Foreign Travel

There cannot be a more fascinating objective to be pursued by an Indian than to undertake travel to Europe or the US. The reasons are obvious. It definitely boosts an Indian's perpetual low self-esteem.

Since travel to a foreign land requires a lot of money, it becomes an important status symbol and display of prosperity. Again, you can attribute the desire for foreign travel to Indian cinema, where the greatest romance and wealth is set in the scenic mountains of Switzerland or on a riverside lunching overlooking London's iconic buildings. These are the 'must see' places for Indians. So much so, that many Indians specifically make a tour of landmarks or places where movies of their favorite film stars were shot. And then they proudly tell friends and family back home that they have seen those very spots.

> **Indians have very poor knowledge of world history and geography.**

It is very daunting for middle class Indian families to find time for recreation; not because they are too busy, but because vacations for longer than a week are considered too long by employers. So an Indian family would not take more than a week's vacation. This would compel them to make the best use of this precious opportunity.

North America and the European countries are more developed and better-organized than India. When compared, India lags behind many other countries in infrastructure, civic responsibilities, hygiene and the state of public property. Therefore, foreign travel for an Indian is not only a holiday; it is a source of amazement too.

As it is, Indians have very poor knowledge of world history and geography, so they are not the deciding factor when they plan trips. The source of information-gathering is the movies, so that it is easy to show off to relatives and friends once they are back. Foreign travel would not include museums, because it would be meaningless to an Indian, except perhaps to see the iconic Kohinoor diamond and other famous artifacts like the portrait of the Mona Lisa. Favorite places to visit in the United Kingdom would be London's Big Ben, Buckingham Palace and Madame Tussaud's, to take pictures alongside their favorite Bollywood stars. In fact, if you visit Niagara Falls, there will be more Indians filling up the viewing points than Americans themselves.

> **Foreign travel is status elevation exercise, providing photo opportunity at iconic places.**

So in these times of a tough economic situation, governments are encouraging filmmakers to produce Indian movies, shot in these tourist locations. In one case, when a blockbuster movie was filmed in New Zealand, the next year its tourism grew by 3000 per cent. Of course, before this movie there were hardly any tourists from India, and suddenly loads of Indians started to head for the shores of New Zealand. For those in government, if you want to secure business from Indian tourism, first allow the shooting of a blockbuster Bollywood movie in your country and inundation of rich Indian tourists will boost your economy.

When Indians are touring, they also like to compare things with something similar back home. Somehow, spontaneously, the great Indian pride kicks in. A typical reaction of an Indian standing in front of Big Ben would be to compare it with their superior Qutub Minar. Another classic comment after shopping in London or New York is to stress the extensive availability of global brands in India. They want to sound as if shopping in Indian malls is the same as in London or New York.

The culinary requirements of Indians traveling abroad are very specific. They have become more demanding to comply with the food they have at home. They carry chili flakes and spice mix to cheekily add to their restaurant food. Tour operators carrying Indians either carry their own cooks from India or include special stops at restaurants serving Indian cuisine.

In order of increasing one's economic status, Indians first choice is to visit Bangkok, Thailand. The next preferred destination if their pockets allow, is to be in Malaysia or Singapore. These are supposed to be cheap holidays, but still add to their social status through foreign travel. Those with lots of spare money visit Dubai to show off their purchases of fancy electronic gadgets, perfumes and gold. If Indians have relatives and close friends in Europe, they do find it easier, but if not, they take a guided tour, typically crisscrossing six or seven countries in ten days. It is more to avail themselves of photo opportunities at popular tourist spots than to know a country. Indians who are serious tourists with plenty of greenbacks, visit the US and Canada.

Since many Indians have traveled to foreign lands over the years, the pioneer effect has been lost. To achieve one up-man-ship, which comes naturally to them, the Indians have now started to explore places which are remote and generally unheard of. The quest for status has sent Indian tourists to countries like Colombia, Guatemala, Chile, Mauritius, Botswana, Seychelles and even Cuba.

Fair Complexion Attracts

Indians are blindly charmed by a fair complexion. I am not sure where this enchantment came from, but it seems to have drastically changed how Indian women and men perceive the idea of being beautiful. My understanding is somehow connected to the British Raj, where the elite and powerful were white or rather fair-skinned. It is this association of fairness with elitist that drives the association of fairness with high standards. Normal Indian citizens were poverty-stricken, working hard under the harsh tropical sunshine which made them look depleted, dark and disheartened. Subsequently, in independent India, the Indian elite emulated British cultural and social habits as a natural progression to improving economic status.

The movies, which are the strongest influencing factor, have actresses looking their charming best with their features Photoshopped cinematically. Gradually glamour became associated with a fair complexion. In the continued trend, all advertisements whether it is hoardings, print or electronic media, there is a good chance to have some 'white' unknown model to depict glamour. The great Indian mythology, the *Ramayan*, also depicts the *Ravan*, the villain, as dark, big and demonic. So here is the initial association of dark complexion with villains.

India is a country of "white supremacists"

Over the years, the complexion has become one of the prime factors in a girl's marriage, as fair complexion is considered beautiful for all these reasons. The boys are seen to go after girls with fair complexion more often than the others. Talking about girls, most Indian movie songs have praised a girl's fair complexion in their description of beauty. No wonder then that mythology, the British Raj and Indian movies all played an important part in designing fairness supremacy in India. We could say that India is a country of "white supremacists".

There are fairness creams available, turning over billions of dollars of business, advertising how fairness will develop over the weeks. One advertisement suggests that a girl got a job offer just because she was fairer than the others. Another advertisement shows a movie stuntman being promoted to replace the star actor because his skin is now fair and bright. One has to be fair to get the 'star look'. If there is no scope for bringing enough fair complexions to a TV show or a Bollywood movie, the producers would choreograph half a dozen girls from Russia or Ukraine to dance in a musical number.

The net effect of this obsession is the extra stare that 'white' foreigners get on the streets of India. When I say 'extra', it means up to ten 'Mississippi' or longer. The stare could be repeated multiple times till the subject feels as uncomfortable as a celebrity in a public place. Some might even stop the work at hand, so that their eyes can follow the 'white' line.

Arranged marriage decision pivot greatly on fair complexion.

Girls and women in general, those conscious of their looks and complexion, avoid going out in the sunshine to avoid a deep tan or dark skin. When they do go out, they wrap a scarf around their head and face, so that only the eyes are visible. As mentioned earlier, arranged marriages pivot greatly on fair complexion. As the Indian marriage system works on resumes and profiles, the matrimonial columns for seeking a bride would mention being 'fair', as a qualification and in the column seeking grooms, would advertise 'fair complexioned girl'. Let us say that it is a complexion suited for marriage. Since being cast in the movies, actresses have worked to lighten their complexion. There are at least a few actresses who had a dark complexion in the initial stages of their career and over the years have done something to become fairer.

India would be one of the only places where complexion can play an important role in deciding the success rate of a person in their personal and professional life.

G

- Guests are God
- Gold Means Everything

Guests are God

In the native Indian language, it is said *Atithi Devo Bhava*, which means Guests are God. In practice, this belief is the foundation of Indian society.

How would the guests be treated? Guests could arrive as being invited or uninvited. They could be well-known, an acquaintance or a best friend, but they are all guests. They could be a close relative or a longtime neighbor too. Long-term guests can also arrive uninvited to stay for weeks and months together. If a close relative visiting the town, wants to avoid inconvenience to the host by staying in a hotel, it would be a recipe for a damaged relationship. It will be seen as derogatory and could cause a permanent rift in the relationship. Even though the house may be small, sleeping on the host's sofa or the floor is more acceptable than staying in a hotel.

Once they arrive at an Indian household, guests are the most significant people for the duration of their stay. They get all the attention. The duration of the stay is generally not the main criterion. From as short a visit like a door knock by a delivery man, to hosting someone for months together, guests are important. It is also disrespectful to allow someone to leave your doorstep without being offered water or tea. Even if it is a postman, over a brief conversation requires the customary responsibility of the addressee to ask for a glass of water.

Guests decide when they want to come and go. They can never be told by the hosts about their unavailability, except when the host is away from home.

Whenever you are offered tea in southern India, it actually means coffee. It is not an option for guests to refuse to eat or drink, although they could pretend to be in a hurry or give the classic Indian excuse of having eaten just before that visit. Refusing to eat or drink (non-alcoholic drinks) would offend the host. Hence, the host just informs the guests that there is tea on the stove, or brings some without asking.

The visiting guests are treated with tea and a snack, usually cookies or home-made savories. The more times food is offered, then insisted upon multiple times, more is the score for honoring a guest. A host's sickness makes a very valid reason for a visit by a guest. This courtesy visit is mandatory if the relationship is to sustain.

Serving food when the guest is formally invited has some specific characteristics of India. The guest would be offended or consider it as sub-standard hospitality if they were served with packaged food. Home-made food is the best for courtesy. The highest accolade in the guest's honor would be if the dessert were also home made. This custom extends to gifting home-made snacks, pickles and sweets to neighbors and loved ones. As a common practice, a special guest will be treated with a dish gifted by the family or a friend of the host. It is a gesture to indicate how highly-valued guests are when they get to relish the equally valued home-made dish from another loved one. It could also mean that the dish has traveled across the cities or is from another country.

If the guests are not from the same city, state or country, the courtesies extended are extraordinary. Many travelers from outside India are greatly overwhelmed by the warm welcome, not only in households but in hotels too. In order to experience this hospitality in its fullest terms, one must stay in Taj Hotels or other five-star hotel chains in India. My personal recommendation would be the Taj Mahal Palace Hotel, Mumbai.

Many a times, foreigners in the countryside are not even charged for small purchases like local tea or coffee because they are considered as a guest of the country. This is true most of the time, but it also depends how well one has interacted with the sellers. Still, it is better not to have it as an expectation. If it is a busy tourist place, then one must be prepared even to be swindled.

Guests in an Indian home outside India receive the same kind of treatment with respect and honor as they would in India. Lots of food and non-alcoholic drinks will be a characteristic. If the occasion is a special one, it will be in culinary overdrive. Guests can be prepared to shut down their own kitchens for the next day as they would have been overfed the previous day.

Types of guest who are very common are:

Short term:

- The chatty neighbor who makes their way over every day, maybe multiple times a day. If one of them is sick, the other one cooks. There are no family secrets and they can be classified as friends.

- Well-being inquirers, who make a courtesy visit to check about the sickness and well-being of the hosts, but still have to be served with tea and snacks.

- Surprise guests, who arrive for a chat just because they were in the neighborhood

Long term:

- Early risers, who wake up earlier than the hosts, so therefore the hosts have to reschedule their sleep cycle. If the early riser guest is elderly, then the schedule becomes even stricter. They would like the entire household to practice their routine and if required they would pursue with a heavy hand.

- The categories of guest that exist in India do not fit into the western classic definitions of a guest.

- For most Indians, it is a measure of good-heartedness and friendliness to have guests all the time, whether they are short or long term. The amazing achievement is that Indian homes accommodate all varieties of personal habits and etiquettes. Many a time, the wife will not know that her husband is bringing friends over for dinner. Impromptu invitations and hosting guests are considered skills which all Indian families have inherited and execute to perfection.

Gold Means Everything

Only gold glitters in India. Most gold possessions owned by Indians are ornaments. They are prized possessions and a measure of wealth and security.

A gift in gold is what one receives right from the first birthday. For every occasion in a lifetime, Indians receive or buy something in gold. So these could be birthdays, festivals, personal achievements, marriage or just casually shopping. On a special day of the Hindu festival called *Dhanteras*, the entire nation floods into the market to buy something valuable which will raise their personal wealth. Obviously, gold becomes the choice both for women and men.

No Gold – No Wedding

As common as the blacksmiths, goldsmiths are a necessary part of any market, be it in a village or a city. They also act as craftsmen to customize jewelry in the local workshop. Usually, goldsmiths are patronized by a family and often would be the family's goldsmith for generations together. Since the purity of gold can be compromised and there is no widespread measure of authenticity, trust and your relationship with the goldsmith is the only way to be sure of real gold.

Following are some global statistics about the passion for Gold in India:

Government and Private Gold Deposit and Ownership (Approximately)

India – 18,000 Tons

France – 2,400 Tons

United Kingdom – 1,250 Tons

H

- Humor
- Holidays – an Indian Meaning

Humor

Humor in India is based on making fun of others. It includes mocking obesity, skin color, age, dress, voice, accent or statehood.

The most popular jokes are based on the English or Hindi accent of people from different states in India. They also joke about contemporary celebrities from politics, sports or films. In Indian humor, it is normal to act as blind or handicapped and have fun with it. It might seem to be insensitive elsewhere, but Indian audiences and the public in general thoroughly enjoy laughing at these painful realities of life. What could be termed as racist in the west is just a sense of humor here in India.

If television soap wants to add some additional comedy to the plot, they would introduce a character who is mentally challenged. The conduct of that character will appeal to the audience's sense of humor. As another example, popular entertainment usually has a character that is dark-complexioned, speaking in a native accent from a particular state of India. All these characteristics are not seen as objectionable, even to the film censorship board or the television content regulators.

These representations have made Indian society very judgmental about looks and special needs, for the purpose of entertainment. The daily soaps in India might look insensitive at times.

Holidays – An Indian Meaning

India before 1947 was a country with widespread slavery. For more than two centuries, slavery was the method of working for large populations, so the idea of holidays and vacations is still not well- established in Indian society, even today. Indians are reluctant to take a vacation from work. Their breaks seldom exceed ten days, as the employer would not be happy allowing absenteeism. My experience of India indicates that taking a leisure holiday for more than five days creates a sense of guilt in employees. They consider themselves to be lazy rather than fatigued.

Although a vacation is intended as a break from work, it usually involves visiting relatives or going on a pilgrimage. Even in destinations which have beaches or nature trails, a visit to a nearby religious spot cannot be ruled out. Also, Indians would want to find a family relative living in their vacation destination. You should understand that Indians choose places for vacation where their relatives live, however distant those relatives might be. In case, they are visiting places where there are no relatives or friends, they take along with them another family or friends. In many instances, even honeymoon trips have a company of some friends or relatives.

If you check with your Indian friends about their weekend plans or vacations for mandatory annual holidays, the answer would not be as assertive as you would like it to be. If at all they are sure, it would be about visiting their close relatives or extended family.

Summer vacation is the time for holidays, when schools are shut for two months. This coincides with overcrowded trains and overbooked airlines. So travel plans have to be made well in advance, up to ninety days, in order to get a reservation on the train. Interestingly, there is hardly any company in India which allows its employees to apply for leave ninety days in advance, that too for ten days or more.

Usually Indians like to visit places with scenic water bodies. There are numerous rivers, lakes and waterfalls, and miles of coastline to lure visitors for Indian-style good times. Somehow, though, Indians seem unable to differentiate between daily bathing and having fun in natural water. It is usual to find Indians having fun in rivers, lakes or waterfalls while also using their shower gel and bath soap.

As well as this open-air bathing, many also wash their used towels in the same water source. Obviously, the bushes and branches of the trees are the clothes lines for the population enjoying themselves there.

Picnics also require people to cook their midday meal at the location of a day out. Taking ready-to-eat food for picnics is not the type of fun Indians understand. Water for cooking, drinking and dish washing is sourced from the rivers, lakes and waterfalls, not to mention using them as open-air toilets too. Cooking at picnic spots is not simple, because of limited kitchen facilities, but food cooked for picnickers is elaborate, celebratory and extensive.

Even though the British are hated for the atrocities committed during their rule, still Indians are greatly fascinated by London. They all want to visit London at least once in their lifetime. It is mostly to pose for their Facebook® page in front of Buckingham Palace, Trafalgar Square, Big Ben and other iconic buildings, where Indian movie directors has used these locations in scenes for box-office hits.

I

- Indian Police
- Indian Railways – everyone owns them

This is one of the famous Indian police jokes. Once upon a time there was a competition to crown the world's best police, with participating teams from the US, UK, Japan and India. The US police claimed to resolve a crime within forty-eight hours. Scotland Yard then claimed to solve it within twenty-four hours. The Japanese proved their efficiency by solving the case within twelve hours. The great Indian police claimed to have known twenty-four hours in advance, when and where the crime would happen.

People could write books on how the Indian police functions in their characteristic way, across different states of India. Well, as we know, the Indian policeman is very powerful and each one of them is a sort of law unto themselves. The actual power varies by rank, combined with unofficial privileges that have been acquired over a period of time. As time progresses, so does their ego. When I say they are a law unto themselves, it means they can walk into a shop, pick up things and not pay for it. They can also eat at a restaurant and walk off without using their wallet. Similar is the case with toll roads, public cinemas, tobacco shops and even the railways. Though India might have signed the UN Declaration of Human Rights, still an Indian policeman can slap, hit, whip or kick people on the road or those in their custody.

As usual, Indian cinema has umpteen scenes to glorify this behavior, starring both debutantes and the greatest of the legendary actor. It is so common that it is an expected and acceptable practice by a policeman. No one even complains about it. If this method is not used, one should be surprised.

Indian Police & Crime:
They always seem to know, why, when, where, who will do it.

It is understood in India that police personnel are poorly paid and therefore they have to make up for this loss of income by illegal means, big or small. Also, there are no duty hours. They work around the clock in freezing winters, steaming summers and torrential monsoons. By western standards, that calls for a millionaire's pay packet on account of hardship allowance and overtime.

Indian policing is a combination of antique and modern approaches. Most of them will wield a wooden baton, usually the length of their legs, or a WWII rifle, good enough to break one's shoulder with its own weight. I am not sure if it really works or is just for intimidation.

Identifying a policeman is easy. They wear a khaki uniform, a shade of brown, which differs slightly in shade from state to state. Do not assume that it is a fancy dress competition if you find someone funny with a gigantic belly falling over their belt. There is a good chance that they are a middle-ranking officer out on a power walk.

Families of policemen are an extended part of the police system. They behave as if they have an official designation. They too can walk into shops and businesses to avail themselves of facilities for free. At times, they can also order things to be delivered to their home. These are associated privileges of being the family of an Indian policeman. The most sought-after is the red beacon vehicle that comes with the job. Even if the official is not in the vehicle, the red beacon is used by family members to evade traffic signals or to get a free pass at the tolls. The children get special treatment at schools or in relation to admissions, which is a struggle for every Indian parent.

Indian Railways - everyone owns them

Indian railways are the heart and soul of the country. If there is one infrastructure outside an Indian home, which still belongs to an Indian, it is the Indian railways. All Indians think that they own the railways and therefore use it with absolute freedom, full rights and complete ownership. While traveling, Indians will sit anywhere, maybe on the seat, or on a space on the floor, or on top of the roof. They will also stop the train with the emergency brakes (by pulling the chain), where they think it is convenient for them to get down. Carrying luggage equivalent to five families is common and at times they also carry their goats, farm produce and gigantic milk cans. They decide when the train is allowed to leave the station, which is only when their friends and family have boarded it. Until then, the train is stopped by putting on the emergency brakes. It is an important instrument for Indian passengers.

Along with being a convenience to get to places, the railway defines the national character. It is the barometer of Indian frustration and at one time, late-running trains were the nation's favorite subject for gossip. In fact, it is often said that Indian railways follow IST -"Indian Stretchable Time". In one instance, way back in the 80s, my night train started from the platform and stopped. As it was time to sleep, I made myself comfortable in the berth for a good night's rest. When I woke up the next morning and my destination looked familiar. It was still my starting station. Since I missed my appointment at the intended destination, all I did was to take a taxi back home. Nothing can match this good night's sleep in the Indian Railway coach.

Although, events like this do happen, but they are a rarity now. What often happen are colossal delays. Sometimes the long-distance trains can be late by six or twelve hours, especially during monsoons when weather disruptions are common.

It is important to know that the Indian railways are the largest in the world, mostly built during the British Empire after 1853. Subsequently, after independence from the British Raj, it has been run fairly well. As you read this sentence, it is carrying nearly twenty-five million Indians across the country. The railways have always been an integral part of the Indian psyche. A good part of the Indian freedom struggle is also associated with the Indian railways. Last but not least, many blockbuster movies and popular romantic songs are filmed on trains.

You will commonly see a few people hanging out of the train coaches and sitting on the roof. It is true; they do so without fear even when the train is running at high speed. A peculiar feature of all Indian trains, which are its doors make it possible. The door does not shut automatically. It is the choice of the passengers to keep it shut or open. So that makes it a useful smoker's point on a moving train or a spot to catch some fresh air while waiting for the toilets to be free.

Many a times, the trains are so full that passengers have to lean out of the doors or travel on the roof. Travelling on the roof is addictive and I, myself have done that many times, although on slower trains. You might have seen those famous James Bond fight scenes on the train roof, but because Bollywood is special, they have choreographed a superb hit song and dance number on the roof of a moving train. To experience this fascinating musical number, search YouTube for *Chal Chaiya Chaiya*.

Toilets on Indian railways are Hooper toilets, where everything falls on the track below. These toilets give the Indian railways their characteristic aroma, both inside the trains and on the platforms. Try to avoid using the toilets on the train as much as possible, because generally they are found to contain human 'masterpieces'.

The railway platform is usually more than a kilometer long, in order to accommodate the length of the train. It is full of activity in anticipation of the train arriving at the station. Although the stop is brief, the volume of people involved in the action is remarkable. The railway authorities at the platform check the authorized passengers and pick up the ticketless travelers. They also make sure that all the goods and services like local mail and parcels, food and services are securely loaded or unloaded. The technicians check for hot wheels, tapping the unreleased brake switch, while other support staff, clean and fill up the water in the coaches. The vendors on the platform cook food in open kitchens and serve it hand-packed, hot and steaming. Passengers try to make sure they grab a cup of hot tea from a platform vendor. There are others who sell toys and items for immediate use, like to toiletries and air pillows. The railway platform also plays host to inventing scented paper-soap, which is a pocket booklet of soap coated pages for the travelers. Each page is for one visit and a booklet cost no more than a couple of British penny.

Depending upon the size of the station, the platform is also dotted with red colored shirts, worn by porters. They are often close to a hundred in a large size station. They carry heavy luggage for those who have traveled and those about to start their journey. Those who are not engaged with any passenger, just wait for the right one.

It would be wrong to assume that they have a trolley to stack and roll the baggage. All the porters in India, just as in centuries gone by, carry the luggage on their head. They grasped one in the left arm and the other by their right arm to balance the load on their head. Sometimes you wonder if these amazing feats of weightlifting would easily win them an Olympic gold. Moreover, the labor charges are not standard and are very cheap. Much like the Indian practice of not giving anything away easy, labor charges depend on bargaining, once at the beginning of the service and once towards the end. Even if someone has wheels on their bags, still the porters insist on carrying it on their heads. Otherwise, he cannot justify the labor for these charges.

There are food stalls which also add to the characteristic aroma of the Indian railways. Most of the delicacies served are local to the city and the region. Absolutely essential is tea and coffee, which is served everywhere. In some places, earthen and terracotta pots are used to serve these hot drinks. I can vouch for the exotic taste and aroma it adds to the tea. Food is served either on paper plates or on a dried leaf molded to make a plate or bowl. Amazingly, even with flowing gravy this innovative crockery is able to hold the local cuisine.

When the train stops at a station, it is fun to watch the thousands of passengers quickly get off. While some end their journey and leave the train, others alight to find something to eat or drink. The time management of the passengers and the food stalls on the platform is remarkable. It consists of finding the right stall with a choice of the right food; buying it and carrying it securely back into the train. The guy at the food counter has to manage so many customers at a time, while he is packing food, handling cash and simultaneously cooking it freshly too.

To add to all this dynamic and chaotic movement in the sea of humanity, new passengers are seen boarding and others leaving the train.. To the population on the platform, add the number of loved ones who have come to greet or bid farewell to fellow Indians. Altogether, there could be a thousand Indians on the railway platform for some purpose.

Except for the air-conditioned compartments, which are just three or four in train of twenty-four coaches, the windows are open so they make it a handy place to transact business while other passengers are sitting inside. For those ladies or elderly passengers who prefer not to venture out onto the platform during that short stop, they can request the vendor on the platform to deliver through the window, or ask a co-passenger to help. Millions of passengers seek this favor every day and therefore, it is part of the Indian railway culture.

Interacting with co-passengers is also an interesting feature that travelers on Indian railways relish. Trotting at an average speed of forty kilometers per hour, co-passengers on a long journey often end up being very helpful, to the extent of managing luggage, giving free advice on business, medicine and tips for safe jouney. , if their destination coincides with yours, for the first time traveler, one can get help on local cuisine and tourism.. People also share their food with co-passengers if they have traveled for some distance. It is common to exchange addresses and phone numbers at the end of the journey and become the best of friends. If you are out on the platform or in the toilet, co-passengers will be glad to mind your luggage, even though the Indian railway officially recommends chaining bags under your seats. There are many friends to be made and subjects of interest to be shared. In short, Indian railways provide a complete experience of typical Indian-ness, in the shortest possible time.

Indian railways are not air-sealed. This means that the windows are a source of ventilation. The coaches have nine cubicles with eight berths each. Each cubicle has two characteristic black colored fans installed on the ceiling. These fans are caged and very close to the ceiling. The amazing fact about these fans is their inability to circulate enough air in those crammed coaches. So they have many other innovative uses.

The person in the uppermost berths is always scared of thieves stealing their footwear in the night. Naturally, this makes the top of the fan cage an ideal place to keep footwear at least within one's sight.

Interestingly, nearly all the fans run perpetually throughout the journey, whether it finishes in hours or days. If a fan is not working, there is one and only one Indian trick to start it. Use your comb or pen through the bars of the cage to gently push the blade of the fan. It will start working and never stop again. This is a time-tested formula and works on all the fans in any coach of the Indian railways.

Shoe shine is a necessity in India and is required at least twice a week. The roads are dusty and public transport is not adequately covered. The shoes become the first casualty of wear and tear. Indian culture has answers to this problem too. There are umpteen shoeshine boys lining up at railway and bus stations.

The shoeshine boys are an integral part of the Indian railways. They are freelance businessmen, who travel on a fixed route.

They walk along the aisle identifying the owners of dirty-looking shoes. You will be amazed to see the shine on your shoes, once their job is done. This service is not legal, but the Indian railways do not mind it, as it creates employment. These shoeshine boys are also seen on the railway platforms, but they are authorized this time. Usually they are sitting on the floor, under the most visible pillar with a characteristic wooden box and a crude anvil. For the customers to wait while the shoes are being shined there is a courtesy (red) carpet or temporary footwear to rest their feet. Customer, big or small, is God in India.

Indian railways come with a unique culture and tradition of bidding farewell. Especially for the long-distance trains, family members and friends come to the station to see travelers off. For every family member who is traveling, add another three who come to the station to bid a hearty farewell. If the person is traveling great distances, and not returning soon, then you can expect even more people who come to bid farewell. There would be children, women, elderly and even neighbors. If a bridegroom is traveling, especially after a recent marriage, the more the number of the bride's family members, the better a send-off it is considered. In fact, it is customary to say goodbye with a large crowd to honor the departing guest.

The procedure for a send-off is simple but well-practiced. The person who is leaving does not lift their own baggage into the coach, if he is not the youngest in the entire crowd. Nor do the women. As the train arrives, the youngest, who considers himself the most capable, automatically takes responsibility for loading the baggage into the coach and identifying the right seat. While this is being done, the departing person stays on the platform and tries to finish off the customary conversations and pleasantries of bidding a farewell.

It is kissing, hugging and the traditional touching of feet, which is the highest mark of respect to elders. If the train's stop is short, for a few minutes only, this event is rapid. As the trains start to move, the smart guy who got into the coach, to store the baggage jumps out from the crawling train. Since there are many in the coach at the time who are not traveling, but just in there to organize things for the honored guests, there is confusion among the passengers as to who is staying and who is getting down.

As these long trains creep away from the platform, handshakes continue through the doors and windows, as they do not like to shout. Usually the parting words are reminders of top priority issues like taking care of the children's education, health and well-being, conveying respect to the other elders in the city, and finally advice to be careful of the luggage on the train. Since the Indian railways are sensitive to this age-old and widely-practiced tradition, the train moves at a slow speed while covering the platform. From an engineering standpoint, the inertia of those chunks of steel railway coaches also compels them to have a sluggish start.

When the train gathers enough speed so that people on the platform are not able to catch up, they wave goodbye and suggest giving a call once reaching the destination safely. It is only when the last coach of the twenty-four coaches, the guard's cabin, leaves the platform that the remaining people start to turn back for home. There is a reason for this wait after the train has left. Many a times, the train moves a bit and even before it leaves the platform, it stops. So the loved ones get few more precious parting minutes to spend with each other. Is it often that the train stops within the platform after initially moving? Yes, it is, because when people are late or not able to board because their food shopping took extra time at that intermediate station, the co-passengers pull the chain for an emergency stop. The guard has to then walk down to that specific coach to release the switch, and then the train starts again.

Day in, day out, in station after station, millions of Indian families and friends perform this routine when they play their part in bidding farewell to their loved ones.

Even today, if the president or prime minister of India flies out of the country on an official trip, even though it might be for a short duration of three days, it is customary for all the ministers and VIPs in the country to give a red carpet send-off. This is something which India learned from British etiquette followed for their royal family. In a way, today, all Indians are treated as royals, when it comes to traveling on Indian railways.

On routes where applying the emergency brakes for personal reasons is frequent, the passengers themselves release the brakes. If the train horn blows twice, it means someone has 'pulled the chain', while one horn means the train is restarting. Across India, it used to be a very frequent practice to pull the emergency chain for a personal stop, but lately it is limited to only rural areas and countryside trains where farmers and students do it for loading and unloading of their farm produce.

J

- Jugaad – Making things Work

Jugaad – Making Things Work

This concept prevails throughout the Indian mindset and is applied to all parts of an Indian life. *Jugaad* is a non-conventional and cheap fix for complicated problems. It was usually applied to engineering initially, but now dominates the national psyche. The concept of *Jugaad* ranges from providing a technical solution in computing, an engineering fix to using a loophole in the law. It is not limited to resolving political deadlock using mischievous methods.

As you know, Indian highways are dotted with roadside eating places, *Dhabas*, which are basic in amenities but serve elaborate food. They serve India's best-cooked regional cuisine at a very low cost. This makes these spots a place for high volumes of customers throughout the day. The *Dhaba* manager has to wash large quantities of fruit and vegetables to cater to those hungry travelers. Here comes the great Indian *Jugaad*. The conventional top-loading clothes washing machines come in handy in providing washed vegetables and ready-to-use ingredients for the cooks. Taking this one step further, the same machines are also used to spin butter out of milk or to make buttermilk from yogurt.

The hotspots of *Jugaad* are in rural India, where resources are limited and people have to make an engineering fix using whatever is available. In the rural area of north India, you will find a home-made automobile, run by a diesel engine which was meant for an irrigation pump. The charm of this vehicle lies in its ability to carry twenty-odd passengers through the rough terrain of rural India.

As the concept is overwhelming, the vehicle is also named a Jugaad. Since it is a home-made automobile, there is no chassis number or registration number. Obviously, the owner need not pay any tax.

In numerous instances, the idea of *Jugaad* comes in handy for the fast-moving, price-sensitive economy. On a crowded bus, where the bus conductor is unable to move in the aisle to collect fares, the passengers transfer the tickets and the fares through a human chain. It is a regular practice and passengers are expected to co-operate in this socio-economic *Jugaad*.

The Indian railways crisscrossing the country, find the farmers hanging their large milk cans outside the coach windows along with their bicycles so they can conveniently carry their produce to their destination.

Paying bribe to get work done is also called *Jugaad*.

This type of innovation can also be seen in homes and on the street where people have used a plastic chair as a WC for the disabled, used the rear wheel of a two-wheeler to run the water pump, or applied a padlock to all three pedals of a car to safeguard against thieves. Children start early on with *Jugaad*. Very often they puncture a hole into the plastic cap of their water bottle to insert a straw, or use paint to make fancy canvas shoes. The ladies are adept at this too. In the kitchen they use glass bottles as rolling pins for making Indian bread and rub folded newspapers to remove garlic skins.

It seems that this sense of *Jugaad* or frugal innovation has also helped Indian scientists to successfully launch a Mars orbiter at one tenth the cost of NASA's Mars mission.

There is widely published literature and books written about Indian *Jugaad* innovations where the authors are trying to analyze how Indian gray matter provides clues to solving complex domestic and global challenges.

K

- Know It All – Only Superficially
- Kite Flying

Know It All – Only Superficially

Indians are highly intuitive and instinctive. Either they know a concept or they are able to catch on to things faster than the speaker. Given just a hint of things, they are able to make the right connections and arrive at the required conclusion, quickly and absolutely. This makes Indians thorough in concept and poor in implementation. It does not matter if their conclusion is even based on facts or belief. They will also push you hard to make sure that you accept it.

It is not uncommon to find each sentence beginning with a "but" or a "no" while conversing with an Indian. These conclusions can be drawn about the topics not even heard of some two minutes ago.

Working with the Indians will falter whenever attention to detail is vital for success. Indians rarely do well at fine detail except when it comes to traditional embroidery and craftsmanship. Otherwise in real-world skills, they are not dependable. Very often you will come across an obese advising about weight-loss methods or a bald taking about stopping hair loss. Many a times the source of teaching and preaching is puzzling.

> **Sports in India are done best by watching on TV.**

This attitude of grasping concepts and only the big picture, without getting into detail, has impacted the country in all areas. If the country India was a business entity, its report card would look brilliant but on the grounds the reality is different. For example, the nation's report card might speak of some thousands of miles of roads, but actually not all of them are worth a smooth ride. Officially it is claimed that every child has a school to go, but those schools might just have one teacher for all subjects and for all the classes.

It is a common sight to find someone with a Master's degree in a subject not knowing even the description of their core subject. A tax graduate not knowing the difference between direct and indirect taxes, an engineer not knowing how a Sat Nav works, a commerce graduates not knowing how business is done. Even today, in rural areas people assume that the Prime Minister of India is good if he can successfully tackle the Chinese premiere or American President in the wrestling ring.

While in-depth knowledge about the subject is a rare commodity still it is a wonder how much the Indians talk to each other. When Indians talk, they have a tendency to stage one up man ship, every time. It is a perpetual effort to demonstrate that 'I already knew it' or 'I know more'. This leaves the Indians as poor listeners, restlessly ready to respond to score a point. Talking to one another is about scoring points.

This makes salesman in India an interesting breed of knowledge and business. While the salesman wants to push the customer to buy, his arguments for product's reliability and benefits surpasses most Nobel winning ideas. These days the use of word 'Nano technology' and 'computerized' is imminent when hearing the sales pitch. When asked to clarify a particular feature, the salesman blabber extra information like 'exclusivity' and 'personal recommendations'. Certainly too many clarifications will blow up the deal. Hence, instead of relying on the salesman, better to be prepared with own homework when shopping in India.

Kite Flying – Not Dreams

Kite flying is another fantastic activity which is still prevalent in villages and old towns of India. On a particular day in January, the entire nation is seen on their terraces, parks and playgrounds, flying their colored kites and engaging in kite fights. The special thread used for a kite fight is made with gum and glass pieces, to cut the opponent's string. It could be dangerous for a novice but it is a complete thrill for audiences and enthusiasts. On 14th January of every year, called *Makar Sankranti*, the sky in a village could be filled with a few thousand and at least a million kites in the big cities. Exciting street competitions and bets fill the festive air along with kites of different shapes and sizes.

Kite flying is just not restricted to one day, but to an entire season. For every generation, there are millions of beginners and novices. As a result you see the kites stuck on the overhead electrical cables. If you are visiting a city and find numerous orphaned kites, dangling on those wires, you are at the right place for this medieval-style entertainment filling the city's sky.

Kite fights do not end when a kite's thread is cut by someone else. As the released kite swings in the breeze, over the houses and parks, children run after it, from one alleyway into another back street, to capture that bounty. Sometimes, if the kite is returned to the owner, they might get paid. Even if not, it becomes a honorable catch and a status symbol.

As a society, Indian poets and filmmakers have used kites as a metaphor for freedom, a happy life and limitless thinking. It is said that electricity could have been discovered in India long before Benjamin Franklin did. They were just too wise not to have done that dangerous lightening experiment.

Since the caste system and economic strata heavily reinforces the social fabric of India, it is very difficult for an ordinary Indian to aim high and achieve big. There are more stories of rags to middle class than rags to riches. Traditionally, Indians are not allowed to dream hence kite flying compensates for the ambition of reaching the top.

L

- Law Breaking
- Living with In-Laws
- Lifestyle

Law Breaking

Indians care less about the law if no one is watching them. Making things legal does not help the Indians. The law is not highly respected in India. In fact, they take pride in finding ways to dodge the law.

Given the first opportunity, Indians like to either break the law or stretch it to the limit. Most survive in a zone which is within compliance, but dodging is equally prevalent. Ticketless travel is an offense which all citizens across the globe would avoid, but travel on Indian railways is a classic example, where millions travel without proper tickets every day. Taxation is another area where Indians dodge the authorities by paying little or nothing. It is a common practice.

Jumping red lights is even more common. During her visit of India, Oprah Winfrey commented that she would like to know if those lights were for fun or from a discotheque. Traffic just starts to creep ahead into the road until the last vehicle in the green lane manages to whisk through. Speed limits are hardly observed, thanks to the overcrowded roads which act as an automatic speed regulator.

A rule book is just theoretical, talking about the law is impractical.

Spitting and smoking are strictly prohibited in public places, but the walls of most public places are colored with red *pan* spit (I explain this habit later). The menace is so out of control that it requires God's pictures and posters to prevent people from spitting on the walls. The corners of the buildings are the usual place where record "spit-athons" can be held. It is worse than the chewing gum menace of the west.

An Underage driving a car is aprevalent sight in India more than children in the west sitting in their baby seats. Million adults in India drive without a valid license too. If they have one, it is either bought or the test was too simple. In Mumbai, the driving test requires you to drive the car on a straight road for less than fifty meters to get the license.

Although the health ministry supervises prescription medicine, it is freely available over the counter. For small ailments like the flu, sprains, back problems, seasonal fever, stomach upsets or headaches, the boy at the chemist shop gives the medicine along with the dosage. All one has to do is describe the symptoms and you get a reliable medication. Surprisingly, they all work.

If an Indian is trapped by the authorities, say for speeding or traveling without a ticket, they raise the idea of 'making adjustment'. In that case, the officer may either reduce the penalty or take a bribe to let them go. There might be some anxious moments, but at the end, all parties leave happy and the law of the land stays intact.

Living with Parents

Reading this chapter title, you are probably thinking that we all do that until we are teens. But I am talking about India, so it has to be more interesting than that.

In Indian culture, a son never leaves his parents' home, unless there is no job opportunity in his home town. The son completes his school and college education and tries to find a job in the same town.. This is so that he can continue to live with his parents. There is no question of having to move out to another house within the same city, as that is not socially acceptable. Friends and relatives would assume that a family dispute was behind the separation. If a son is ever separated from his family, he brings dishonor to the family name.

Family honor and pride is a big deal in India. The opinion of society matters to everyone and is one of the major factors affecting any decision-making. Separation, even for the sake of convenience and privacy for newlyweds, will be viewed as evidence of a family feud. The ramifications are severe and would affect pending marriages in the family. A daughter who is next in line for an arranged marriage will have to take the brunt of this family dishonor. The prospective in-laws would discredit or give a lower rating to the girl's marriage proposal.

It is well-known to every bride that she has to treat her in-laws like her own parents: look after them, cook, laundry and do their other household chores. In real life this does not happen quite so smoothly though. The other two chapters in this book, 'Old Age and Retirement Homes' and 'Living with In-Laws' relate to this chapter.

Living with In-Laws

When she is married in a traditional way, a girl leaves her parents' house and moves in with her husband and the in-laws. If they are all in the same city, she might be living not only with the parents-in-law but also with co-living brothers and sister in-laws. If there are sons in the family and they are married too, then they all together make up for one large joint family. There will be a common kitchen where all the women will cook together for the entire family. Resources are generally shared, and this cohabitation takes another generation into its fold.

Every member of this large family will have differences from time to time, but will adapt their ways to continue living together. This is a typical Indian joint family system.

It has its disadvantages too. I know of several cases where people have found it very difficult to cope with the joint family system. On the other hand, its advantages seem to outweigh the benefits of the nuclear family system. It is not that a few separate family units are living together; instead it is one large family living under the same roof. The members of the family look after each other in times of sickness, in times of need and when emergencies strike. Expensive baby-sitting is not required, and nor is day care for children. There is always someone around to talk to and share with. The house is never empty, which might be why depression and Alzheimer's are not so prevalent in India.

Some interesting facts about living in a joint family after an arranged marriage include time management and the allocation of resources. All members of the family would have individual routines, but they all integrate harmoniously with each other. The couple might not get much private time, but they still find a way to make babies. The men, and more often the women too, leave the home in the morning for work and when they are back they gather with the entire family for dinner. Privacy is in short supply when compared to the western lifestyle. The couples in a joint family hardly have a chat because there is always some other family member around. In a joint family system, going in your bedroom during the day to talk to each other is considered rude by other members.

> **In Joint Family System, Expressions between wife and husband is limited to only bedroom.**

This is the norm in a joint family and nobody complains. People do not consider an alternative until space is too cramped and something affordable becomes available in the neighborhood. My friend has two children in the same house and has raised them into grown men. She will get them married off in a few years' time and their two brides will also join in to make a bigger family. This cycle of family life will continue. It is very typical of India.

Lifestyle

Here are a few assorted bits and pieces of characteristic Indian lifestyle.

Pronunciation

Indian languages are spoken as they are written. Words do not have silent letters and are pronounced no differently than they appear to be. Therefore, when an Indian speaks any other foreign language, they sound out all the syllables. For example, the alphabet, 't' in the word is very prominently spoken. *Restaurants are pronounced as Res-tu-rants*. Even the word 'pronunciation' is pronounced as *pro-noun-ce-a-tion*.

As there are 29 states, each with a language of its own, it gives English language the honour to be spoken in 29 different accents.

English is an unofficial national language. Indian assume, being the largest English speaking population in the world, it gives them the democratic right to call their pronunciation the right way to sound words.

From Stranger to Extended Family

Stranger -> Acquaintance -> Friendship -> Close Friendship - > Extended Family

Here I would like to share a real story. A friend of mine travelling on an overnight train journey had a co-passenger with a broken arm. As any other Indian will do, my friend helped him with his luggage and food box. To pass time, the two started to chat about generic topics and global issues. At random, the co-passenger indicated to my friend about his boss's house hunt. The two shared details about the property market in the location of my friend. The journey came to an end. Each gave contact details to the other and went on with their business as usual. Days later, the co-passenger's boss contacted my friend and to keep story short, co-passenger's boss became my friend's neighbor. The string of friendship continues even today, after more than a decade when they all first met in those unusual circumstances. They now exchange visits and seek each other's wellbeing. It is an extended family of my friend, the co-passenger and his boss. The amazing fact is they are living in three different continents. This is not a usual incident but an indication of how Indians interact.

Indians are very quick to form relationships, and take quick steps to create an extended family. In a typical human relationship development in the west, the same shift from being a stranger to being part of an extended family would take many years (often it will never happen). With the chatty Indians it is a matter of fifteen minutes or just meeting the same person twice.

They all establish connections through gossip and general topics such as health, politics, children, income or movies. The relationship matures through co-operation in terms of childcare, vehicles, mobile phones, maternity, dress and appearance, text books and school recommendations.

> **Never say 'buy lunch'.**
> **Always 'invite'.**

Still stronger ties would develop from participation in marriage ceremonies, birthdays, choosing grooms and brides and suggesting medical treatments. In a friendly relationship, it is very offending to keep track of money spent on each other. Going Dutch to a dinner is insulting, even mentioning it would be offending. When people from other countries ask for 'buying lunch', Indians in their heart feel slighted. As a culture, Indians are 'invited' for lunch.

Time Management

Two or three days, one or two hours, or "As Soon As Possible"

It is no surprise that Indians have poor time management. From being marginally late to a meeting by few minutes to reaching a location a few hours late, if traveling by road and by years if it is an infrastructure project, there is a component of slipped time commitment. Rarely, does a public meeting of national leaders start on time, nor does a live TV debate come to an unrushed timely close.

It is an Indian practice to wrongly declare VIP's time of arrival at the event. If the VIP arrives at the location in time, it is a good chance that the audience would not be complete and the event management folks are still working. So, it makes sure that VIPs are informed about a delayed time of arrival than the general public. Very clearly, Indian wants to distinguish between 'coming' and 'arriving'.

If an Indian journalist is conducting an interview, certainly they have to rush up towards the end to close the show. The allocated time is never enough. It is always two more questions after asking the declared 'last question'. You will even spot this talent with best and top TV journalists of India.

Thrifty, not miser

Indians are not really misers but they are rather thrifty. They have difficulty in throwing things away, especially if they are made of plastic. Instead, they find innovative purposes for used things. For example, a toothbrush never retires. After the toothbrush has finished its service of brushing the teeth, the owner uses it as a brush hair color. As the bristles further wear off, it is then promoted to cleaning brush to sweep the corners of machines, sinks, wash basins, strainers, dishes, etc. After retiring from this job also, when the bristles have really worn off, the brush stick then finds a use in threading the pajama cord. Indian pajamas do not have elastic to hold them around the waistline; instead they have a cotton string for a secure hold on the waist. This journey of the toothbrush is a classic example of reusing domestic and industrial things, multiple times till the economic value has been squeezed out of it into junk. When compare to developed countries, the junk comes much earlier in the life of an object.

Superstition

Once a land full of snake charmers, India still has the weirdest of superstitions to ward off bad omens. The main doors of the houses are always adorned with various auspicious objects to attract good luck. These would be images of Gods and Goddesses on either side of the door frame. The symbolic footprint of the divine marks the center of the doorstep with the sign of the Swastika, OM, or 786 on the top of the door frame. This is to let people receive an automatic blessing as they pass underneath for their daily business. Many Indians also install Holy Scriptures from Hindu mythology, the Holy Quran or the Bible. These scriptures have figurines of ornamented horses, elephants, bells or the holy cow.

Some methods of warding off bad omens include:

- Black spot on the left temple or forehead (especially children)
- Lemon and green chili mini-garland on the edge of the doorway and the rear view mirror

- Breaking a sacrificial coconut on all happy occasions, like the champagne at a ship's launch

- 'Shani Oil' worship on Saturday

- The Swastika, Cross or 786 on doorways, gates, account books, safe lockers

- Horseshoe atop the main door

- Monster masks atop the house

In addition to superstitions are predictions of good and bad things that might happen, with cues from unrelated things. They are called *Shagun* for good and *Av-Shagun* for bad events to happen.

A few examples of indicators of good things coming soon are:

- Spilling boiling milk
- A flower falling on the floor of the home temple
- Left eye twitch

A few examples of indicators of bad things to come:

- A black cat crossing the road on your journey
- A mirror or glass breaking in a marriage
- Sneezing right before an auspicious ceremony
- Oil lamp flames of the home temple, going out
- Right eye twitch
- Rainy day on a Diwali

There are many more symbols of good and bad omen from various places in India and they all are very interesting.

No Sorry, Thank You or Please

Indian society is very relaxed in etiquettes and people like to interact in a most friendly and informal style. This is also valid while interacting with strangers too. Indians rarely want to use words like "Sorry" or "Thank you". These words are used only in very formal settings like hotels or by call center agents.

When saying sorry, it actually lowers the self-esteem of the majority of Indians, while 'thank you' distances an individual from social closeness. When Indians try to incorporate others into an extended family, it is unacceptable to repeat these words of courtesy, which are deemed to be imported from Britain. If a native speaks these words to a fellow Indian, they might attract sarcasm about being British. But these courtesies are well accepted from a white foreigner. See, I told you earlier in the book that Indians are white supremacists.

Handling embarrassment

Whenever Indians want to provide information which is formal in nature or could be embarrassing, they like to speak in English. For example, when asked about work or education , the reply is often very formal and scripted, but in English. Similarly, when talking about adult topics like pregnancy, menstruation, etc. that part of the conversation will be in English (even though only one sentence). The entire conversation before and after that sentence would remain in native language.

Daily Newspaper

All Indian households subscribe to at least one daily newspaper. This newspaper is delivered every day at dawn, to their doorstep by the newspaper boy. The Indian man's morning does not start without reading the newspaper. If the delivery of the copy is late, other than because of bad weather, the matter becomes serious. The interesting part of the newspaper is not what it publishes but the use of newspapers after all the sensationalism has been extracted. The papers are collected in the corner of each household as scrap called *raddi*. Periodically, a scrap collector will knock at the door of each household to purchase the old newspapers. The lady of the house, traditionally responsible for the sale, bargains with the scrap collector. If a deal is struck, he weighs the stored old newspapers and magazines with his rudimentary weighing scale. While this goes on, the lady of the house keeps a close eye on the procedure or asks her smartest kid to do so. This game of outsmarting each other is played out every few months on the doorsteps of millions of Indians. Amazingly, it is all for a bounty of two or three dollars at the most.

While the used newspaper is waiting for its rightful collector, it comes in handy as tissue paper to wipe spilt water and milk. Nearly all households make the newspaper into shelf liners and drawer mats. In order to keep the crease stiff, it is used as an insert in freshly-ironed garments. While the west uses its latest invention of microfiber cloth for cleaning windows, Indians use newspaper to wipe their glasses sparkling clean.

Mostly, Indian families do not use a tray when having a cozy snack in the bed. What better bed sheet protector can there be than multiple layers of Indian print media sitting underneath their exquisite Indian cuisine? Many shops still use newspaper pieces to serve takeaway food. Probably the printer's ink just adds flavor, if nothing more.

Eating groundnuts are a favorite way to pass time and bond with co-passengers in the trains and buses. The uses of Indian newspaper are unlimited. The groundnut seller packs the ground nuts and the accompanying mix of salt, pepper and chili flakes in a pouch made of newspaper. Also, the passengers traveling on buses and trains use it to collect the shells of groundnuts.

Idea of Hitler

Indians like decisive personalities, who have demonstrated clear leadership in their fields. Often Indian history is punctuated by political leaders whose followers have grown to extraordinary heights. Few known decisive Indian leaders include Lal Bahadur Shastri (Prime Minister, for winning 1965 war with Pakistan), Indira Gandhi (Prime Minister, for winning 1971 war with Pakistan and creating Bangladesh), Atal Bihari Vajpayee (Prime Minister, for developing nuclear arsenal to counter Pakistan), Kapil Dev (Cricket Captain, for winning first world cup), Sachin Tendulkar (Cricketer, for breaking nearly all records in cricketing history), M S Dhoni (Cricket Captain, for winning world cup cricket), Narendra Modi (Prime Minister, for development model) and Arvind Kejriwal (Fire brand anticorruption crusader).

For the same reason, Hitler is not a forbidden name in India. Indians when frustrated with non-responsive governments wish to have a decisive dictator like Hitler to set the systems right. There is a good chance that a bookstore will have a copy of "Mein Kamf' in display and people flipping its pages with interest. Further a premium TV channel runs a daily soap called 'Hitler Didi' which portrays the protagonist, an elder sister, as very strict and strong, pursuing discipline. This reflects two things, firstly that someone who is strict and imposes discipline is nicknamed 'Hitler' and secondly Indians have a very poor appreciation of the world history.

Conversations and Compliments

When an Indian has to start a conversation, they inquire about the obvious. A typical example would be to ask if "you are watching television now". This is something which is clearly visible for anyone who has entered the room. For close family members arriving home, it is usual to say "Have you come home?", as if the answer could be "no". This question is commonly asked and answered sincerely, even though it is so obvious to both participants.

Giving and receiving compliments is not part of the Indian lifestyle. It is very difficult for an adult male to compliment a lady for good looks or dress, even if they are well known to each other. If by great effort and overcoming inhibitions, one does compliment, the receiving end will be too cold (sometimes even ignoring) and might not be worth the effort. The art of complimenting is restricted only to poets and lyricist that too for the purpose of romance. Generally, compliments and appreciation are in short supply in Indian society. It comes with suspicion for looming gains. Also, Indians are taught to remain grounded and those who seek compliments are high headed.

Others
- The pressure cooker is a must in an Indian kitchen. They would even carry one to the Antarctic expedition.

- The typical Indian adult male likes to carry in his pocket a pen, his glasses, a handkerchief, a small comb and his mobile and wallet.

M

- Marriage as Festival
  - Marriage procession
  - The marriage itself
  - After marriage
- Maids and Helpers
- Mobile Phones
- Mahatma Gandhi
- Modernity and Development Redefined
- Medical System

Marriage as Festival

Indian marriages are just not an event, but a lavish festival comprising of at least a dozen events. It is considered a sacred union of two families, witnessed by hundreds and sometimes thousands of guests from both sides of the family. This would include the participation of the bride's family, the groom's family, friends, relatives and the extended family of both the bride and the groom.

In a heart rendering belief which marks all Indian marriages, a marriage is called *Kanya Daan*, which means donating one's daughter. The bride's parents traditionally donate their daughter to the groom's parents in the marriage ceremony amidst religious procedures and community rituals. Once the father or bride's maids, as the case may be, had walked the bride, thereafter, the daughter is assumed to be a precious possession of the in-laws. Henceforth, in obedience to the belief, forever, the bride's parents do not accept any materials from the groom's family. This means that traditionally speaking daughter's parents don't even eat food or drink water at the groom's place.

As mentioned in other chapters, Indian life revolves around the family, which is a natural outcome of marriage. Early in a child's life the emphasis is on finding a suitable match. Family members tease children about their match, or parents scold their little daughters against getting scars on their face, which might affect their marriage-ability. All-important life decisions and activities undertaken are connected ultimately to marriage. Girls are kept indoors and not allowed to roam in the sunshine so that a suntan can be avoided. The darker the skin, the lower-rated is the marriage-ability of a girl. The consequences of having a tan and dark skin are discussed in the chapter, 'Fair Complexion Attracts'. Similarly, boys are told to seek a profession which will fetch more in dowries from the bride's family. For example, boys living in the US can demand a higher dowry. Dowry exists in all sections of India, irrespective of religion, caste, community or economic class.

Dowry is a sensitive issue in India and can be a real and continuous problem in the life of a girl's parents.

Marriage Procession:

The groom arrives in a procession as if to win his bride. Indian marriage processions have a hybrid spirit of elopement and celebration, arranged by both the bride's and the groom's family. It is like the fairy tale of a prince who came galloping on a white horse to pluck his princess from the clutches of the enemy. This actually happened in the eventful history of India. In 1175 AD a great king of north India, Prithviraj Chauhan, chiseled his romantic and iconic elopement into the history that has become a model to emulate by ambitious Indian Romeos.

Indian marriage ceremonies, though very festive, are all about pride and stroking the ego of the guests from the groom's side. Though marriage is considered a union of two families, it is viewed as such if, and only if, the bride's family played excellent hosts to the groom's entourage on the day of the marriage. The entourage consists of hundreds of merry making humans, in an age spectrum of new born to century old. If that does not happen for some reason, the bride has to take the brunt of her family's failure in the decades to come. The bride would be reminded frequently in a sarcastic tone, about the shortcomings on that important day, more often than not, how trivial they might seem to be.

A significant event of any marriage in India, irrespective of religion, is the aforementioned marriage procession. Even acquaintances are invited. The marriage procession has many essential components such as the decorated horse, on which the groom sits but does not ride, a mobile orchestra (band) of twelve to sixteen members, with instruments like the saxophone, trumpets, flutes and violins, a lead singer and a gang of dancing friends leading the procession of other groom's guests. The procession is called a *Baraat*, which is also the collective name given to all the guests from the groom's side.

The *Baraat* walks through the street, mostly at night, up to the bride's place. In modern times it starts from about a kilometer away from the marriage place. This is to allow the groom's guests to dance up to their heart's content. The *Baraat*'s orchestra, also called 'the band' in jargon, has its members dressed in formal attire, as if it was the King of England's entourage. A groom is supposed to be treated like a king. They play Bollywood tunes, and if the band has a singer, it is an added feature.

The music is loud, to tell the world about the marriage. It is much louder than the stipulated legal decibels, but the law does not apply in the case of a *Baraat*. Since the *Baraat* makes its way to the place of marriage only at night, the procession is fenced by two dozen men carrying fancy Vegas-style flashing light gadgets on their heads, powered by a generator trolley, following behind the procession. In between the position of the musicians and the groom's pony, are placed the drunken guests of the groom, dancing their hearts out. Since dancing is not practical while the procession is moving, even at a snail's pace, the *Baraat* stops at various locations for the friends and relatives to dance to a particular number. That dance number could be on request, but given the known set of Indian marriage dance numbers, everyone knows which one is coming.

While the procession moves ahead through the street, the traffic is managed by volunteering relatives from the same crowd, who automatically take this responsibility. They take turns between frantically dancing and responsibly managing traffic. The traffic, on the other hand, moves slowly, squeezing past the *Baraat*. Those in the traffic, pop their heads out of their vehicles to see the face of the groom and assess the wealth of the groom's family. The quality of music being played by the band, the lighting accompanying the *Baraat*, the makeup and luxurious dresses worn by the ladies and the gentlemen in general, all reflect the wealth of the groom. The groom's face is partially hidden behind the veil which is a feature of the ceremonial turban. The best men are the ones who are most drunk and dancing enthusiastically.

In India, the best man and the bridesmaid have the freedom to wear whatever they choose. While dancing, they are supposed to throw currency notes in the air, in order to remove bad omens from the marriage and express their joy. The frenzy increases as the procession nears the bride's venue. The beats become high-pitched and the dancing of the men and the women reaches a crescendo of vigor and vibrancy. Other members of the procession, who may not be dancing so frantically, may include the groom's grandparents, parents, and other elderly men and women. Everyone is expected to dance in the *Baraat*.

Nagin Dance

No marriage procession is complete without a *Nagin* Dance. It is an adaptation of classical Indian dance depicting the way snake charmers tame the lady cobra. In Hindu, Buddhist and ASEAN countries, the snake God *'Nag'* and the Goddess *'Nagin'* are revered as a sign of fertility and prosperity if treated well. They both can also bring disastrous results and ill luck if not honored with prayers. Over the ages, as mythology has taken a back seat, people have found fun in the dance, especially after some blockbuster Bollywood movies have pulled record breaking crowds.

In the *Nagin* dance, one man dances with lateral undulation posing as a lady snake while the other, dances in the rhythm to pose as the snake charmer. It is the typical tune played on *Been* or *Pungi* which is a snake charmer's wind instrument. The expertise of the dancers lies in the extent to which one's body undulates with the rhythm. The music has a characteristic high pitch swinging sound which engrosses and overpowers the dancers and audiences alike.

Once the procession concludes at the marriage venue, the mood dramatically changes. From a fun and frolicsome atmosphere, with the loud sounds of drums, the band, and Bollywood music, it changes to sober and religious fervor. All the members of the *Baraat*, even in their hundreds, are welcomed by the bride's relatives with the bestowing of money and gifts. The grandparents, the parents and other important elderly people are given special treatment and a warm reception at the gate of the venue. The groom, being the center of attraction and the chief guest, is very special. For his welcome, camphor lamps are circulated around his body, from head till toe, by the ladies of the bride's family. He is greeted with rose petals strewn on a red carpet, a sprinkling of rose water, candles and of course the throne-like seat, where he will wait for his bride.

The groom must walk down the red carpet aisle with a few thousand waiting guests observing this royal walk, amidst sparkles, sprinkles, and the soothing music of the double-reed oboe (*Shehnai*). On the stage, the public ceremony of the exchange of garlands takes place once the bride walks up the aisle. Up to this moment, all major religions have the same practices for the *Baraat*, but subsequently the private ceremony differs for a traditional Islamic, Christian or Sikh wedding.

As an Indian, just for these few moments of special treatment, attention and honor, one would love to tie the nuptial knots. The groom is the focus of attention and appreciation, with special dress, headgear, food, and flirtatious attention from a dozen bridesmaids. While the bride's family continues to play host, the bride is treated as an enchanting creature, and receives the utmost respect and care. Every now and then, a lady member of the family can be seen adjusting her veil and the drape of her gown, or rearranging the gold and precious stone accessories, with which she is loaded.

The Marriage itself

The marriage day is a day packed with activities, which may start as early as 5 a.m., depending on the auspicious date and time. With the priest doubling as an astrologer too, he derives the date and time after matching the horoscopes of the couple-to-be. A priest without astrology is unsuitable for the profession of priesthood. He suggests a suitable date and time precise to the nearest minute for all ceremonies which involve religious practices. Except for one or two marriage activities, all the events are religious and therefore must conform to auspicious dates and times. The most sought-after accuracy is the time for the exchange of garlands. Failing to do so at the right time raises fear of bad omens influencing the future of a happy married life.

One can imagine the precision that goes into planning events in the marriage festival. If the fear of bad omens were absent, probably marriage festivals would go on indefinitely. Planning does not usually exist in Indian practices. Everyone works on everything.

There is a pattern within chaos on the day of the marriage, where the elderly keep giving urgent directions and the younger ones run around to do the errands. In the midst of chaos, the women demand things which they have forgotten to buy, or which are not working. Visiting a home on the day of a marriage is like visiting a place experiencing an earthquake. In particular, the home of the bride would easily define the word 'chaos'. Relatives and friends are involved in hectic activities of arranging and participating in religious ceremonies. People communicate by shrieking and most of the work is done by verbally demanding it. The air is filled with phrases like "bring that", "take this", "where is this?", "who has that?", "move it", "time is short" etc.

The groom's place is little more restrained and calm on the day of marriage, even though there is a heightened sense of hectic activity. There is a reason for this calmness. The bride's side is supposed to honor the groom's family and friends, including their guests. Therefore, all the heavy lifting and running around is supposed to be done by the bride's family. This includes being highly respectful and majestically courteous to the guests, relatives and the family of the groom.

The role of different family members

If it is understood that an Indian marriage is about the marriage of two families, it is because different members have a specific role to play in these religious events. For example, the bride's mother's brother is the person who either walks with the bride or picks her up in his arms like a child, to take her to the altar for the marriage. Thereafter, the parents of the bride give away their daughter. The bride's brother has the responsibility of traveling to the groom's place just before the marriage procession, to tie the turban for the groom. It is a ritual which is accompanied by prayers and the exchange of gifts.

There is hardly a marriage in India, which does not have an annoyed guest on the groom's side, for not being treated well by the hosts. Sometimes, annoyance can escalate to a dogfight between relatives on either side. A marriage still continues with all this verbal battle in the background. Though it is a happy ending for the couple, everyone knows that they have to go through this drama.

In villages, the rules about marriages are even tougher. The groom's side is strictly treated like royals. It does not stop there. In the case of any deviation in the respect and honor shown to the guests, there could be a scene like something from the Wild West. Guns and swords could be drawn, and this might even break up the marriage itself with a walkout.

After Marriage

An important event in the marriage is the farewell of the bride from her parents' home. This is usually in the morning after the marriage, and involves very high emotions associated with separation. The groom, best men, parents and other elderly people participate in this event. The bride, bids farewell to her siblings, parents, the elderly, servants, pets, neighbors and other close ones. Everyone has dramatic parting words to convey to the bride. The classic ones come from the elderly, who never fail to mention that they did not realize the little baby girl they cuddled and played with, would soon grow up to be a bride. This is a compulsory speech (well, sort of) scripted in all marriages, even if the girl was fifth in line to get married. These sentiments are common to all marriages, irrespective of religion.

Another classic scripted speech comes from the groom's parents to the bride's parents: "Don't worry; we will treat her like our daughter". The farewell would not be over if the bride's parents did not mention this to the groom's parents: "We have raised our daughter tenderly with utmost care. In case she makes any mistakes, this is an advance apology. Please forgive her". These parting words have become so standardized that you can anticipate them in any Indian marriage, and hear them in Bollywood movies.

Tears flow in abundance as the bride walks her way out to the groom. All the while, he is waiting in his car, which is fabulously decorated with flowers. The climax to the marriage is this farewell drama, and it can be really heart-rending.

The bride steps into a palanquin (called a *Palki* or *Doli*) carried by six or four men who can be either brothers and cousins of the bride. The *Doli* and *Palki* were types of legendary vehicles in ancient India. They belong to a class of wheel-less human-powered transport. In medieval India, a palanquin or *Palki* was used as essential wedding transportation. Brides were carried to the bridegrooms' places by palanquin. It was also used as the conveyance for noble Indian women, and for Indian landlords of that time. In ancient India, the palanquin caravan used to traverse miles across the villages and kingdoms for days to reach the groom's house. These days the distance has been shortened to few ceremonial steps.

Thereafter, it is the modern age automobile and flying machine which take the bride to the groom's house.

Once the farewell formalities are complete at the bride's place, the entire focus of the ceremonies shifts to the groom's home, where both religious and fun events take place. This includes the reception of the bride. All the groom's guests who attended the marriage are invited again. The couple receives another round of gifts and the spotlight while the guests have the opportunity to enjoy themselves again. If the guests have traveled from a distance, they receive their fare along with some gifts. The same happens to the bride's guests too.

Maids and Helpers

No Indian household can survive without housemaids and helpers. In the west, it is understood that royals have dozens of servants and butlers, so in that sense, Indians are royals. One can see several servants in a household, helping to accomplish home chores. In most households, even if there are not many servants, at least one will definitely be employed.

These servants cook, clean, make beds, do the laundry, wash dishes, iron clothes, etc. Getting all this done by a servant or a fleet of servants is not considered a luxury in India. Usually the job description for servants is loosely defined or does not really exist. The employers do not want to introduce a watertight job description to avoid conflict with measurement and monitoring. There is also no fixed weekly time off. Instead, all work breaks have to be agreed and approved by the lady of the house, or it might affect the monthly salary.

It would be a surprise if someone earning a decent income in India did not have a housemaid. These maids also look after small children and the elderly at home. It is the reason children are rarely sent to a day care center.

The hired help does not charge hefty amounts for their services. Their charges are so affordable that they are not even worth a discussion here in this book. But still it is part of Indian culture that women do negotiate rates with the maids. No matter how rich the households are, the lady of the house attempts to negotiate lower wages for their maids, driver or other servants. This is not with an intention to save money or any other economic reason, but to avoid being exploited or taken for granted.

Since we are talking about maids and servants, it is to be noted that there is no training the servants have to undertake to be qualified. Some of them work in different houses to gain experience, while for others it might be a new job. The newer ones learn the skills on the job, if hired, but rarely does any recruit want to accept being a novice. Anyway, even if they have work experience, it does not help much. Every lady of the house has their own unique set of instructions to get the home chores done.

Irrespective of the educational or financial background of the lady of the house, she picks on the maid for trivial things. It is part of the Indian culture to micro-manage things and feel dissatisfied with the execution.

Maids are a major preoccupation of an Indian lady. The issue is so prevalent that many household ladies start a friendly conversation with their friends with status of their maid's uninformed absence, or her sloppy commitment at work. On the other side of this excitement, there is astonishing creativity in the reasons that maids quote when they justify the cause of their absence. Death of a near and dear one is the most common which usually get caught. A visit to a doctor for herself or a family member is the next best reason while excuses like responding to a government survey, water shortage, disruption in public transport, late night home coming from a marriage and many others list in the top 10 reasons.

There is no easy way out, because small entrepreneurs and multi-nationals alike have tried to tap into this market of India. They have used their international experiences and management models for providing consistent services but have had their fingers burnt.

The maids are not there just to do the household chores. There is lots of value that maids bring to the relationship other than accomplishing the household work. They bring news from the neighborhood, the insider information that no one else would be able to know. This would mean you get first hand reports of other people's household secrets, affairs, wealth proportions, health issues, eating and drinking habits and not limited to new moving-ins and move-outs. Many times maids carry advance intelligence about the neighborhood, which comes out true with amazing accuracy. It is said that maids knew about the second trimester, some seven months ago.

The fun does not stop here. The fun is when some random neighbor stops by to ask your well-being that was confidentially enclosed within your home address.

I would conclude that while handling maids is a typical love-hate relationship in India, only the lady of the house is the ultimate boss. All other attempts to tame the art and science of household management, are a failure. For westerners, it is impossible to grasp that maid and servants are not a luxury but a necessity in India. It is said that 'Maid in India' is more important than 'Made in India'.

Mobile Phones

Mobile phones have leveled the socioeconomic structure of India. In the country that is still run by social and economic hierarchies, mobile phones have threaded their way through those rungs. While mobile phone numbers may be private, in western civilization, it is your identity in India. Anybody can ask for your mobile number and you can also ask for theirs without inhibition. After a brief introduction between strangers, if you are required to reconnect, or even if not, mobile numbers are exchanged as a courtesy. Subsequently, if the purpose demands, expect a call, even at odd hours.

Mobile etiquettes are not many and simple. In business, keep it short as much as possible, hence no unnecessary pleasantries to begin with or long goodbyes. You should start and end in a moment, with an effective way of conveying a message quickly, breaking all rules of telephone etiquette. All the more important is the frequency of mobile calls an Indian makes or receives. You can see plenty of Indians talking on their mobiles, so it is not an exception; it is a way of life. People are found talking on their phones while driving, eating at restaurants, cooking, working behind the cash register, serving customers at the supermarket, sweeping floors, walking the dogs, watching TV, in the movie theaters, boarding planes, in toilets and even when playing with kids. On an international flight, Indians are the first ones switching on their mobile, immediately after touchdown while still taxiing, If their hands are not free, it is their neck and chin that holds the mobile, while their hands are busy doing other worldly tasks.

If a face to face conversation is interrupted by multiple mobile calls, the other person will not bother to seek an excuse. The mobile phones are also responsible for a poor attention span of Indians, which cannot be more than 30 seconds when face-to-face, 45 seconds over the phone conversation and less if on-line chat. While you have a serious conversation with an Indian, he/she will keep saying 'Yes' or 'hmmm' without looking into your eyes. There is no method or technique to draw their unhindered attention. Well, breathing and talking on mobiles do not require etiquettes in India.

At times, this habit could be annoying to those traveling from the west. Let us just take it as an occupational hazard when dealing with Indians. Most Indians, including celebrities, will be seen carrying a mobile. I am not sure how it works in their bedroom, though.

Making a mobile number public is a necessity. Office culture promotes sharing mobile phone numbers, to stay connected. Do not be surprised to receive calls on weekends or late in the evening for official purposes. While it is important to openly share mobile number, even on visiting cards or e-mail signature, equally important is to respond to the call, otherwise it may be considered as rude. So it is not a surprised see someone publishing their mobile numbers on their Facebook® profile, Twitter®, blogs or other social media.

So much is the obsession with mobile phones that even those who are not able to key in a name to the address book owns one. It is enough for them to know that the green button is for receiving a call. In case they are stuck with the complexity of the device, it is simpler to ask the nearest person, even a stranger, to dial a particular number from their paper diary.

For those Indians who have mastered the use of mobile technology, one hand is perpetually occupied by a mobile. They are either texting or holding it in their ears. The generation in their teens and twenties, text a lot, while the others relentlessly talk. Soon the country will have a genetic mutation of bent necks.

We have heard of driving and texting, but the Indians have a novel way of riding and talking. Boys sandwich their mobiles between their helmet and ear to continue talking while riding their two wheelers. It is an innovative way to skirt the law and still stay connected, while keeping the ride interesting.

Equally important to understand is that mobile phones in India do not have an active voice message service. Therefore, in order to reach someone, it is either text or repeated calls until they respond. Leaving just a missed call is not a guarantee for a return call.

An Indian mobile can break the perfect silence with a fancy high pitch tune anytime at all wrong places. Few of the examples are like the office meeting rooms, temples, cinema theatres, operation theatres, public toilets, yoga class, meditation sessions, railway coach in the middle of the night and many others. One only wonders how someone can keep their mobiles turned on. There is a catch here. Receiving calls mean that one is important and busy which means an upgraded social status.

Necessity is the mother of all these inventions, and inventions have become a necessity in India like no other place on this planet. People with low and even very low incomes still communicate with mobile phones. They give a 'miss call' to the person who can afford a call-back. This concept of "miss call" communication has caught the imagination of more than 900 million mobile subscribers, with a million being added every month. TV channels, political parties, non-governmental organizations encourage a 'miss call' to register a message. It can be as simple as an 'all is well' message to a friend or even approving a national agenda. It is a way of communication adopted by millions. Who in their wildest dreams thought that millions of mobiles would be used to communicate without talking?

Again, how can topics, conclude without a mention of Bollywood? Mobile phones in India double as radios. With over 200 FM stations, earphones are seen dangling from those million pairs of ears because they are tuned into a radio station hearing their favorite Bollywood songs. Although productivity may not be the best at work with those romantic songs in earphones sandwiching an Indian brain, it certainly makes them happy and cheerful.

Some inventors in those mobile companies have an odd sense of observation. They created a flashlight in those mobile devices and sold them in India. In a country where electric power is as erratic as the traffic, people use their phones as a torch. Indians are able to navigate through the dark and muddy lanes of the villages, peep deep into their office drawers, find a keyhole or even replace a fuse wire in an electric power circuit. The best use of a mobile phone torch is to find a matchbox to light a cigarette. Who can beat that innovation?

It is important to understand that millions in India cannot read or write in any language. That they are able to use mobile phones to make calls is a miracle by itself.

Mahatma Gandhi

The toughest job for an author describing India is to write about this great soul in a short chapter, or for that matter in a whole book itself. We are talking about the father of the Indian nation and someone whom international leaders revere and like to follow. He is a reference point in India and around the world, for measuring the objective of living standards, personal spending habits, the politics of principles, sustainable economics and peaceful social norms. Many take his ideas as devout followers, while others like to find fault in his ideology.

If someone is a Gandhian, it would mean practicing prohibition on alcohol and smoking tobacco, eating non-vegetarian food, on partying as in discotheques, with loud music or random sex with multiple partners. Instead, following Gandhi promotes equality of humans, a life of austerity, discipline and honesty, with habits like waking before dawn, vegetarianism, non-violence and practicing penance and spirituality.

While the Gandhian ideals are taught and referred in homes, paradoxically the country works differently. India has become a hotbed of bribery and corruption. Interestingly, Indian currency notes have a picture of this saint. So every time a bribe passes between hands, this saint would be turning in his grave.

The state governments are official licensees and distributors of liquor. Even worse, Indian politics are based on caste and religion. Mr. Gandhi would be wondering if the Indians have read it wrong when he propagated an anti-caste system. Through the eyes of his numerous statues, the Mahatma sees Indians flaunting wealth. If the count is right, the number of pictures, statues and portraits of the Mahatma in the country may by far exceed those of any other human in the history of mankind. Yet his ideals and principles are completely ignored in his home country, in so many ways.

Modernity and Development Redefined

The idea of modernity in India is rapidly catching up and in the last decade has surpassed all previous decades of change. According to the Indians, following the west is being modern. Being modern is not out of necessity of anything else but to elevate social status of being one step ahead.

Doing away with fasting based on lunar phases is the easy casualty. Typically, an Indian would fast at least two days a week, but that may come down to maybe one day a month. It is not that people start losing their faith, but to proclaim that in the journey to modernity, self-restraint from food means nothing.

Modernity in India starts with wearing jeans. Indian men have switched from their traditional custom stitched trousers to faded and torn jeans.

The womenfolk also switch to jeans and a T-shirt, as the first sign of modernity. The next step to becoming a modern Indian woman would be sacrificing the length of their hair. It is cut short to shoulder length, or even shorter to match a western fashion statement.

For every step one takes into modernity, it is assumed that your economic and social status is also rising. This would also mean increased usage of English language, though as partial or complete sentences. Often an accent is used which is from somewhere in the Atlantic, neither British nor American. It is very easy to get that accent. Anyone can have it. Just tighten the lower jaw while speaking English and you are one step up the modernity ladder. Additionally, in an effort to be posh and contemporary, Indians speak their native language with an Atlantic accent. When being in the company of friends and relatives, it would not be right to communicate in that accent, so where is the right place? When hailing a taxi, not at the railway station, but at the airport is the ideal spot to flash your 'Atlantic' accent. Also, they like to talk to the poor cab driver in that accent. The places where Indian womenfolk show off this speaking style is with vegetable vendors, shopping malls or the call center agents.

Swear words along with American slangs are the latest trend in adopting the concept of modernity. The accent may be an added feature and if a teenage swears with an accent, fluently enough, such that no one in the vicinity understands, modernity is considered to have reached its peak.

Women taking up cigarette smoking in public are another sign at modernity. If the global brands of spirits and wine have started to find a place in an Indian home with a classic bar-like display, modernity has really arrived at that home. Wine glasses and the women of the household partying with alcohol can be considered the climax of Indian contemporary style.

If the use of forks and knives in a restaurant is being posh, their use in the household is considered as being western and hence modern. If the use of flat footwear is a necessity in a rapid and chaotic lifestyle, high-heeled women's footwear shows modernity. If eating home-cooked food or restaurant food is traditional, then ordering a pizza or hanging out at fast food shops makes Indians up-to-date and in touch with the current times.

Wearing brand is the new measure of development. In the last twenty years, the country has seen flooding of global brands, whether it is apparels, personal items, automobiles, white goods, consumer electronic or other household items. Today, there are stores for luxury brands like Armani®, Louis Vuitton®, Versace®, Bvlgari® and others. According to an Indian, everything that is available in the west is also available in India and that is 'development'. So there is this strong bonding between brand and development.

What is a Brand, according to an Indian?

Ask them the meaning of the word brand and they would provide an astounding number of definitions. One of the classical definition is "If the goods are available in a fancy shopping mall, then it is a brand". This definition floored me and ripped me off all my academic qualifications.

Surprisingly, even those whose annual income is less than the price of one item of those luxury brands, still possesses it. The Indian market is also flooded with counterfeit and sometimes it can develop an inferiority complex about the 'genuine' luxury brand that you possess. It is quite common to see people buying "Fakes" taking them as original brands. This is because large sections of Indians do not know how to validate a genuine brand.

Medical System

There are countless doctors and pharmacy shops around the country. Every street has at least one doctor's clinic and a pharmacy. In other words, there is always a doctor's clinic and a pharmacy at a walking distance from your home. It sounds pretty amazing, because India produces nearly a million medical practitioners a year. Most medical services are private and nearly all of them are reliable. Like other things in India, medical practices have their own Ripley's® factor.

India is a melting pot of western allopathic medicine, Indian Ayurvedic medicine, homeopathic medicine, naturopathy and home remedies. Then there are the practices of yoga and massage, which run through these lines of treatment. These options are available to all, either discretely or in combination. As the influence of western-style medical treatments is growing, so also are the others.

Most common are home remedies combined with Ayurveda. They are assumed to be grandma's recipes being followed through ages. They are most effective for ailments like colds, flu, constipation, cuts and bruises, headaches and backaches, blood pressure, diabetes, hair fall, graying of hair, dipping eyesight, obesity and many others.

Ayurveda is an ancient Indian medical science which has caught up with the Indians only recently. Not only has the Indians started to practice Ayurveda, they all seem to be experts. The reason for its gaining popularity is its simplicity of formulation with household food . It can be either an oral or external administration. Then the effects of Ayurveda get compounded with the gossips of success stories from the extended family and neighborhood. Most Indians, though believe in this system still seek western medicines to cure themselves.

When visiting a clinic, if outpatient treatment is needed, most cases can be walk-ins, but there is a queue. Depending on the popularity of the doctor, the queue can be from a few minutes to few hours. Interestingly, the outpatient queue is short during festivals and longest during the monsoon season.

The prescription by a physician is hand-written and when you take into account that they write a few hundred prescriptions in a day, it is overwhelming. The handwriting is always illegible and only the local pharmacist near the physician's clinic can actually make out of the contents. On the social side, pharmacists are considered experts in deciphering the doctor's prescription. They can also suggest prescription drugs and at times sell them too.

As the awareness of oneself has grown, people have started a lot about health and well-being. Now this makes them equally curious about their own bodily functioning. The best way is to call and order a blood work all by yourself. The pathology company's call center can guide with permutation of choices and suggest the most suited. What is coming is most interesting. The samples are collected at home the very next day and the reports are available the following via e-mail. One can get a physical copy a day after. The reports are self-explanatory indicating the normal range along with the actual reading. Thereafter, accordingly their home remedies or other medical attention can follow.

I have seen many voluntarily walking into the radiology shop to get their X-ray done. The part of the body which has to take the rays is indicated by the patient and recommended by the X-Ray operator. One may not have any health issue but may rather be curious to know if all is well inside. Again, the report is instantaneous with a casual advice to formally visit the doctor or not. The medical science in India is not left to only medical practitioners but freely available to all in the true spirit of freedom and liberty.

Medical secrecy is an alien concept. People talk about their ailments and other's ailments in the open. Even if the other person is not present, the entire disease can be discussed. In a neighborhood, the gossips among womenfolk might include the medical conditions of some other unknown neighbor. If the name of the neighbor is not known, it is their house number that will be used for reference in the gossip. There is a great possibility that a person in the neighborhood might be identified by his or her medical condition only.

Hospital records are also discussed openly and very often a nurse can be seen explaining the line of treatment to a patient while others are present. If someone is visiting a hospital or calling up the hospital reception to know about the inpatient, it is a good chance that you will be directed after identifying the ailment and the patient. "Is your patient the one with a head injury?" This is contradictory to the practices in the west, where the medical history is not discussed even with the partner without permission.

N

- Names of Indians
- Non Resident Indians (NRI)

Names of Indians

One challenging characteristic feature of meeting an Indian is remembering his or her name. Not only they are difficult to pronounce, they are also very lengthy. So why are the names so peculiar?

As religion plays a key role in everybody's life at every moment, Indians want to stuff their kid's name with as many God's name as possible. The alternative to a God's name is the name of one of his ornaments, traits or nature. This serves the purpose of reciting God's name every time someone calls out the name. While, the name is strongly believed to bring natural protection to the person who owns the God's name, every recital makes people closer to God, gaining credits to be in heaven.

Typically, an Indian name is split into three parts. The first being their own name, the middle name being the father's name and the last name is the name of the village or caste or family name. Now this order can be reversed or mixed up depending on the state of origin. Some Indians try to make their names simpler by shortening the parts of the names with abbreviations.

The trick to remembering names, if they are lengthy is obviously finding the approved short form. Most Indians have one and if not, they will be obliged to provide one. Please don't risk, yourself picking or making a short form. It could become demeaning at times and might do more harm than the intended good.

It is a tradition for everyone to have a home name and official name as used in schools and records. These home names sound very different from official names. The home name may not always be short of their full name. It could be just any other name like Guddu, Raju, Chintoo, Sonu, Monu or even the name of an Indian sweet. The use of these names is so prevalent that many in extended family might never know the official name.

Although, the corporate culture does not subscribe to the practice of using the home names, as in the criminals' world, it is a practice to use the home name. So when police issue the search warrant, they have an alias. These aliases are really funny, contradictory to their heinous crimes. Though it is not scientifically proven, the alias gets funnier with the intensity of the crimes committed by them.

Naming convention in India is typically easy though resulting in complicated names. They all have mythological names depicting Gods from various stories, intended to bring good luck and divine blessings.

The same naming convention continues with other things in the society. The housing societies are named mostly after God, if they are not upscale. So is the case with the names of the shops and establishments. The moment the owners wants to position themselves for upscale and posh market, they name it with some English name like Orchids, Valley, Heights, Woods, Estates etc. While the large government public buildings like airports are named after icons from history, the airlines continue to name themselves differently.

The interesting feature of the Indian naming convention lies with the cinema theatres. Most in the earlier days were named after mythological characters associated with art and dance. At one time, nearly every city in India had a cinema theatre named as 'Nataraj' which symbolized the powerful God Lord *Shiva* in dancing form. All theatres did good business before they were hit by the videos. The same theatres revived themselves and metamorphosed to multiplex theatres with more modern and fancy names.

Non Resident Indians (NRIs)

Those Indians, who are working and living abroad with foreign citizenship or with long term residence permits, are considered as an extra evolved breed of Indians. They are mostly rich and responsible for importing Indian brides in bulk to countries like US, UK, Canada, Gulf countries and others. NRI is sought after by brides seeking groom and also Indian companies seeking investments in their venture. On the other hand, NRIs export lot of exaggerated stories of development and heavenly lifestyle in their country of residence. So when they visit India, they are loaded with international brands and gifts for their loved ones back home. It would be a surprise if they don't have an English accent that resembles to none.

Since they are a hybrid of native and foreign culture, the persona can be classified as both interesting and sometimes comical. It is less for the natural habits one inculcate because of foreign land, but more because of their extra effort to be Non-Resident Indian'. It makes them exhibit a habit which stands out among resident Indians.

NRIs feel hotter in India and complain about pollution as soon as they land at the airport. They look for international brands for food and drinks and many a times may ridicule the local brands for poor quality. Asking for bottled water is a must. Comparison between India and their current country of residence is central to all conversations.

They all get special status among friends and relatives, especially if they are visiting for the purpose of attending a marriage gathering or family function. Many a times they become "trophy guest".

O

- Obsession with Tea & Coffee
- Office Meetings
- Old Age Home & Retirement

Obsession with Tea & Coffee

Drinking tea or coffee is a national pastime. Indians love these drinks less for the taste, more for gossip and excuse to take a break from routine. For Indians, it is tea (or coffee) time, all the time. Even for coffee drinkers, it is called a tea break.

Indian geography can be informally classified by its tea or coffee drinking population. The north, east and west of the country is traditionally tea drinkers while people of south India are coffee drinkers.

The method of making tea is different from what we see in the west. Indians brew tea, which includes ingredients like black pepper, cardamom, ginger, mint, cloves, fennel, holy basil, bay leaves, rose petals, cinnamon, etc. I think Indians fall just short of putting the complete spice garden in their tea. People living in the extreme north of India, in the Himalayas, also add a little butter with a pinch of salt. In my quest to know what good Indian tea tastes like, the answer was not clear. Instead, I found that tea is considered good when it has a strong aroma of spices, served close to boiling temperature, has a color as bright sun tan with a balanced taste of all those spices. Last but not least, tea must be served with respect and courtesy. It is not considered courteous to put the cup/mug on the table when serving. It has to be handed in the hands of the guest, who then can may place it on the table because it is hot.

Although the British are credited with introducing tea to India, it is the Indians who have triumphed in developing it as a national drink.

When drinking tea on a daily basis, it is amazing to see the standard type of shot glass it is served in. Often you find a roadside tea stall where the server brings you tea clutching five glasses in their five fingers, like a honeycomb. In the same way, servers retrieve the empty glasses. Usually it is a young boy called the *chhotu* or the little one who serves tea and retrieves the glasses in the roadside shops.

When I traveled to the western Indian state of Gujarat, things were a little different there. While the wealthy tea drinker prefers stainless steel tumblers, for the general population the style goes a step further with creativity. They serve the tea directly in the saucer. There is neither a glass nor a cup, so the least hassle. In the rush of things, people do not want to use their grey matter on balancing a cup over a saucer and handling multiple things. When the job can be done with just one why bother. Generally, drinkers hold the tea saucer to their lips and slurp the hot steaming tea with a most satisfying 'Aaa-ha'.

In the southern states, coffee is the main drink. It is also the state where coffee grows in abundance. Preparing coffee is much simpler than making tea. It is a mix of coffee powder, milk and sugar. The complicated part, also responsible for the flavor, is the intervening step after preparation and before serving. The coffee is interchanged between two glasses, a few feet apart, at a rate of a few times a minute, so that the air blows through the liquid. Like an expert juggler, the chef swaps the coffee between the glasses. A good measure of the distance is the space between the chef's arms spread out. One glass is empty and the other has the semi prepared coffee. He then restarts to pour from one glass into another, while again increasing the distance between the glasses to his arm's length. The liquid is frequently interchanged between the tumblers as the jugglery continues a couple of times until the coffee gets frothy and suitable temperature. The act is a public display and not a single drop of the precious drink is spilled.

That is how tea and coffee are served differently as traditional drinks in the northern and the southern geographies of India.

Corporate India is no stranger to 'tea culture'. Although there are imported fantastic machines in the pantry, still the employees walk across the street to the roadside tea stall. These stalls are called *Tapri*. They are very basic poverty-driven shops which also sell loose cigarettes and condiments. Still, the quality of tea served, though in rudimentary shot glasses, can beat the tea from a luxury five-star restaurant.

These *Tapris* are spots similar to the water cooler, where talking, gossips and bonding happens, as in the west. If people do not have an appetite for tea, never say no to an Indian invitation. Instead, opt for a 'cutting,' which is a serving of half a cup. It is expressed in the jargon of Indian tea culture.

In cities where information technology companies are clustered, these spots are also a good information exchange for exploring greener pastures.

Office Meetings

Work, as in any other country is chaotic and filled with meeting schedules. In India, meetings rarely start on time, unless the chair is strong-headed and keeps the flock together. In that case, he would be the most hated. The agendas are diverse and wide-ranging. If there is a meeting with a focused one-point agenda, then it is not considered worth having a meeting at all. Usually, the solutions are already known before the start of the meeting unless it is about some complex global issue like the Iran nuclear program, the crisis in Syria, civil nuclear deal or next president of the US. I would expect solutions to these are also known in advance.

As said earlier, the agenda is usually longer than the time allocated for the meeting. Although much is discussed, equally much is left to be discussed the next time. Even the best of the national TV channels struggle to complete their talk shows.

When two Indians interact, it is less to understand and be understood, but more to reinforce their own knowledge and hence the solution. There is nothing that really counts as discussion. For every pronouncement on a topic, discussion is termed an argument and conflict creeps into the interaction. If the discussion is outside the office, on some political issue, there could even be verbal abuse and violence. If you accept the argument, well and good, or else one can be bracketed as misunderstanding. Never use the word 'disagree', or swords (virtual ones) could come out easily. It is simpler to agree and take the topic in a completely different direction. That is acceptable and neither spoils the meeting, nor the relationship. If a meeting of Indians starts on time, and ends on time with all the agenda completed, then something is wrong.

When there is no element of struggle, it is leisure, which does not justify the pay packet. Well, meetings are required in leadership roles and not really for the lower rungs in the organization. A high position in an organization gives a higher justification for meetings. If a senior officer is not in a meeting and is easily available, then it is assumed he was not working hard enough. A one-to-one meeting is not called a meeting. Usually, a meeting would include many employees with an agenda that is assumed to be complex.

Asking too many questions in office meetings does not go down well with Indian culture and Indian bosses. Sooner or later one might be branded dumb or a rebel who is questioning authority. Instead, in case of doubt, it is to better ask a colleague later even if it was 'meaning of an acronym used'. The rule is, do not speak until asked and always start with "I agree", even if the statement shows completely opposite opinion.

There is little scope for discussion in a meeting as most of the decisions are imposed by the boss with a pre-decided outcome.

Old Age & Retirement Homes

It could be surprising how this works in India. To begin with, the concept of retirement homes, senior living and care homes for the elderly is almost non-existent. The home for the elderly is their own home, which they built and spent their lives in. They do not have to go through the pain of separating from their belongings and memories associated with them. If you talk about an old age care home, Indians would think of a shelter or refuge for the homeless and abandoned elderlies. There might be only a couple of western-style old age homes in the metros.

It is considered children's failure if they cannot take care of their own parents. Ask any Indian how they care for their parents and grandparents. Does it affect their normal life? Their argument is both touching and realistic. They want to know if any parents blamed their child's birth for the changes to their work, sleep and budget. Old age care is very sensitive and considered as a sacred duty of young ones to fulfill. So, why parents should be put in a care home when their children are alive?

It is very difficult to understand how year after year; an Indian family will look after their bedridden parents even if it lasts for a decade or even longer. Most of the nursing is done by family members. In critical cases, they create a family roster for round the clock attention. Doctors are requested to visit the parents at homes if required, which they do in most cases. The family may even create a mini hospital at home if required. Those elders who are very old and have no near ones to take care, it is the neighbors who are the dear ones to attend. They take the responsibility to support the household errands.

Another fact is that an Indian does not have to make arrangements for their own funeral funds. The children pay for the funeral. Even if the family is poor, it is a social responsibility of children and neighbors to provide a decent funeral.

Compare that with the situation in the western world, where it is common to see advertisements, usually in the mid mornings. They suggests ways to save money for one's own funeral. In India as long as a person is alive, no one ever talks about dying, or funeral of self. It is considered insensitive and inappropriate. If any elderly were to talk about their funeral, they would be indicating to their children how useless they turned out to be. In particular, planning for a funeral is absolutely out of the question. So much is it taboo that people do not even write their Will document.

It is not surprising that the finances of a deceased person are found to be in a mess, as it is never discussed with the family. Even questions may not be asked about whether they will be taken care of properly. It can happen that no one in the family knows where all the money is invested, which all bank accounts it is deposited, how many credit cards the deceased had or the loans he owed. I have seen families struggling with bank details, passwords, claiming the life insurance, etc. But that is still not a valid reason to talk about the Will document with family members when someone is still alive. It would be taken as an indicator that they are waiting for their death, or that the children are concerned about their inheritance, a little too early. Not only do Indians look after the elderly, but they also give them all due respect and attention. Arguments with the elderly, disobeying their wishes, and speaking in a loud tone to them is not welcomed in Indian culture. It is also considered a sin.

Typically, the retirement age in India is 60 and has not moved since 1998, when it was 58. Government employees, who are retired, use their last designation, with the suffix as 'retired', if it adds to their pride and status. Irrespective of the designations, all retired undertake self-administered routines like morning walks, excessive newspaper reading, extensive financial planning and increased level of religious indulgence.

This arrangement sounds unbelievable to us in the western world. But it works out very well in India. As an economy, taxpayers do not have to pay for the care of the elderly and citizens themselves do not have to worry much about their own old age care. The approach to the concept of age and the aged is astonishingly dissimilar and can be a cultural shock for people of both hemispheres.

P

- Parenting - Never-ending
- Privacy
- Philosophies of an Indian
  - ➤ Pride
  - ➤ Honor and Respect
  - ➤ Fate
  - ➤ Status
  - ➤ Help
  - ➤ Sharm or Haya
  - ➤ Karma and Seven Lives

Parenting - Never-ending

Once a child is always a child in India.

Indian parents want their kids to be toilet-trained as soon as possible. As diapers are not common because they are costly and carry waste, so parents want to avoid it. Proactive to prevent soiling, they train their babies to associate tinkle with a whistle. Generally, children start indicating their need for nature's call within the first year, itself.

By the very nature of the civic facilities, pram is unusable in India, so babies are carried in arms for hours together. This makes mothers want their children to start walking as early as possible. Consequently, Indian babies as early as two years old can be seen walking alongside their parents in a marketplace.

Like the diapers, the concept of baby food is not much in practice. After the initial period of six months of breast feeding, parents hold a ceremonial religious feast, *Annaprashan* to signify other food for the baby. Thereafter, children start eating adult food along with milk.

Babies become babysitters as soon as another younger one comes into the family. It is a common scene to find a seven-year-old carrying a one-year-old in the arms, while the parents are occupied with their work. As soon as possible, the elder one starts taking responsibility, and if it is a girl child, she becomes an automatic help in the kitchen. A daughter can be her mother's help by the age of seven. In the villages, it could be still earlier.

Parents teach children much more than you would expect for their age. This means that before beginning their first day at school, children know how to count up to three digits, some nursery rhymes, the identification of colors, stories from mythology and biographies of national personalities. Some might be able to sing the national anthem or devotional songs. If there is a guest visiting a home and there is a child, it is mandatory that parents demonstrate the newly-acquired abilities of their child.

As they grow up, checklist of hobbies and recreational activities make up the middle class children. With the rise of consumerism and a wealthier middle class, parenting has changed more towards the provision of facilities. These days' parents ferry their children to school, tuition, painting class, karate coaching, tennis coaching, swimming pools or dance studios. Since all these options are now available in a changing India, parenting means enforcing every option on their children. Children are also being swamped with gadgets and fashion apparel.

One of the parent, usually the mother become the ferryman. With the traffic choking the Indian roads, children take a nap while commuting between classes. All this is to make the resume of children lengthy and impressive. Whether naturally the child is inclined to a particular hobby for real gets answered only after five years, when the results start plummeting when hobbies advance to higher levels. By the time the children grow up to teens, they are left with either one or no hobby to pursue.

It is a common sight in India to see children playing in the streets and parks, on their own. Also, in the metros, one can find young ones travelling on trains and buses without any adult supervision.

Parenting in India can be much simpler than anyone assumes. If the child is conforming, everything is fine, otherwise scolding, slapping or whipping is used to gain compliance. Slapping is one of the widely-used methods and can be done even in full public eye. It is not something to be ashamed of. As a culture, parents can slap their children right up until they are teens, but thereafter scolding is the preferred method for the rest of their lives. An Indian can be scolded by their parents in public, in front of friends or family members alike. It is not considered embarrassing to either of them. In fact, this treatment is a feather in the cap for any child for being highly respectful and honoring of their parents.

There is no age when parenting stops. Parents can intervene in their teen children's university education, judge their friends, criticize their dress sense and approve suitable sources of entertainment. In particular, parents are greatly involved in marriage decisions and subsequently in the successful running of their marriage. They can provide expertise in areas of conflict management, following traditions and major buying decisions like that of a new home or vehicle. Parents are responsible for marrying their children off, especially daughters which come after struggle to find a suitable match.

As it is an acceptable part of the culture in India to scold or slap children, Indians living abroad do get investigated by their local authorities for being violent and abusive. Adapting to new cultures and laws might take some time, but change does come to Indian parents living abroad. Things then get interesting when visiting grandparents try to use their own expertise in handling their grandchildren. Keeping with traditions practiced for decades across generations, has proven that old habits die hard. Many a time children have innocently called the emergency number, with some justification, to complain about their grandparents.

It has been a long-standing idea for parents to decide on a child's career path even before they have started counting up to two figures. Like their neighbors, suitable career choices are being an engineer or a medical doctor or running the family business. A family business might also be running a law firm, a construction company, a hospital or even a music school. Whether the child has an aptitude is the least concern of ambitious Indian parents.

It is a common saying in India by the parents that you should be an engineer first and later decide on a career. Many 'Engineers' do not put their engineering knowledge or skills at use during their entire career. It is not surprising to find engineers in business management, public services, hospital administration, financial services or even politics.

Schools are known for their extended parenting. Teachers can use any of the three methods of discipline, of course with limitations. Many a time, parents complain to the teachers for being too lenient with their kids and recommend increased strictness.

The Indian police also think they are parenting the wider population of the country. Their first step in disciplining citizens is by using these primitive techniques. They can slap and shout at subjects in the full public eye and it is an acceptable norm. Indians think they are lucky if they can escape without going through this at least once in their lifetime.

Privacy

Privacy is difficult to find in a country that is seriously overpopulated. It is crowded in all public places: cinemas, trains, roads, buses, hospitals and schools. So where does one find privacy?

Traditionally, there is no concept of privacy, because of the habits and lifestyle of Indians. Privacy has been rare in the country, as families live in a joint family system. It means that most space in a household is shared by its members. The only place left in the house for some privacy is either the bedroom (only in the night) or the restrooms. Who would want to be in a bathroom just to have some privacy?

A joint family includes members of all ages, from newborns to ones from world war era. This results in limited access to privacy. In a joint family, everyone knows everything about the other family members' business. It is discussed openly in the living room in both good times and difficult ones. It would include sources of income, actual income, health issues and their remedies, taste and preferences, progress in school, menstrual cycles and other issues. All this information would not usually be known in western society, let alone be openly discussed in the living room by family members. Even if family members are not living together in the same house, still these topics are not private. Once you share something with any one family member and call another family member after 15 minutes, they would already know it too. It is the same practice among Indians living and working abroad. If you tell an Indian something, even with a note to keep it within the four walls, chances are it will be shared with their close Indian colleagues, with a note to not share with anyone else. This makes Indians very indiscreet in conversation and at times can end up being intrusive or overbearing. It leaves little room for the concept of privacy, both in terms of physical and mental space.

In case a member of a joint family is hesitant to share, while others are openly discussing things, such silence would start to look like being secretive and arrogant. Importantly, Indian society allows its most senior members, mostly grandparents, to be informed about everything in one's own life. They are honored and respected to possess worldly wisdom from experience. Failure to share not only leaves the younger members devoid of expertise and wisdom, but subsequently they can be branded as rude and rebellious. The fear of these negative labeling results in disregard for privacy and a necessity to be completely open. No one will never hear an Indian saying "Please leave me alone". Being 'alone' is the last thing an Indian would like to do.

By definition, 'solitude' is the closest that one gets to 'privacy', if translated into the native Indian language Hindi. So when Indians talk about privacy, what is meant is that people change their clothes is in solitude, although Indian men and women have tricks to be able to do so in public, as well.

I also know that summer is the time where a large population sleeps outside their bedrooms, on the terrace, as a community. Like all readers, it is surprising to me too how so many children, still are born in India.

In the western world, where data like medical records, credit card information, banking information and others might be private even from the spouse, it is shared and keeping secret is considered derogatory in India. So Indians living abroad are often found to be frustrated with this arrangement.

Although the Indian banking system is trying to adopt this method of data privacy, still they are very lenient when practicing it. Most of the wives would have never operated a bank account as it is a purely man's task. Moreover, it is also considered as too complex for many ladies who are either tied up to the household tasks or not educated enough to understand the banking procedures.

Philosophies of an Indians

Indians do things to align themselves with fundamental philosophies like trust, pride, respect, honor, and fate. These are not standalone philosophies. Instead, they are intertwined, such that all transactions, whether social, economic, emotional or commercial touch them all. Most TV commercials appeal to the sentiment of trust and honor. It is a general reflection of Indian society's mindset.

Here are few examples of each.

Trust:
Their work culture is based on trusting relationships or *Vishwas*. Even for a routine transaction, as small as taking a cab or running family errands or doing the daily shopping, right up to setting up a large multi-national business, creating a relationship is central.

This means treating another person as part of the same family. It might sound strange, but very often you find two strangers transacting business or sharing information about finance or health by proclaiming that "it is matter within a family" (*Ghar ki baat hai*). If you happen to go twice to a grocery store or a restaurant, or hire the same cab driver twice, they become part of your family. The security guard of your apartment building will be extra careful in watching your apartment while you are away. He will help you carry your heavy suitcases in the elevator and put them in taxi for you, for no extra tip or charge. You will be guaranteed extra attention and privilege which might soon culminate in sharing information that is more than just formal pleasantries. The same percolates down to all Indians as a culture.

Since dealings, are based on relationships, mutual trust naturally creeps into interactions. People might exchange useful information about local happenings, the prices of goods, recommending a doctor, cooking tips, the cheapest deals, health tips, safety precautions and even dress sense. All this and much more one can get from a couple of friendly interactions with a stranger. Quite often Indians travelling on a long-distance journey on an Indian railway arrive at their destination with wisdom that is not to be found in books. The relationship develops very quickly and becomes quite a close one, which most people from the west would take years to achieve. I have learned most of my worldly wisdom from taxi drivers or the doctor or the housemaids or sometimes from a co-passenger on the train whose face I no longer remember. This is also one of the reasons that people share all their problems, experiences and stories with so many people. Who knows someone has already found the solution to the problem I am dealing with right now?

The founder of the Daewoo group, Kim Woo-Jung, called his autobiography 'Every Street is Paved with Gold'. I would suggest that every Indian street is paved with golden wisdom.

Traditionally, Indians do not need to verify with any scientific or academic evidence for recommendations given by friends and family. They base their judgment on their personal relationship with the person who is providing the information. It might be a matter of yoga, health, and car maintenance, the durability of goods, religious practices, home medicine, a restaurant, a political leader or even a marriage proposal. It is possible that a particular matchmaking could happen based on the recommendation of the family doctor. And it works well too. Unlike in the west, where every aspect of society is based on scientific research and evidence, debated and discussed in multiple public forums, Indians follow what is said by an assumed authority, either in the family or in a social circle.

If someone's daughter is more than twenty years of age, automatically neighbors, friends and relatives start suggesting a suitable match even when parents have not yet decided to marry her off. The same applies to sons. Immediately after they start earning a decent income from their job or business, matrimonial matches start pouring in from all sources. The neighborhood is part of an extended family and hence mutual trust.

Running a business with trusting relationship requires the blurred boundaries in the job description. The idea of a job description is useful only when working outside India. In Indian organizations, strictly following a job description may hamper the employee's growth and the employer may not entrust with crucial tasks. In order to grow, an employee must accept whatever is assigned and obediently works upon it with full commitment. 'It's not my job' is seldom heard.

Pride:

Pride, or *Guroor* in Urdu and *Garv* in Hindi, comes to an Indian with great difficulty. There is a religious and spiritual factor in this behavior. The nearest translation of the word 'pride' has some positive connotations in the English language, but it comes with negativity in Indian languages. Translations of the word 'pride' are linked with arrogance, so children are taught to avoid taking pride in themselves. But there are many other areas where Indians do take pride.

The Indian does take pride in highlighting inventions and discoveries from ancient India, which western science glorifies as scientific discoveries. The Indian scripture of *Hanuman Chalisa*, from 3000 BC, accurately measured the earth's distance from the sun. Another significant example is the discovery of turmeric, ginger and garlic having anti-cancer properties. For Indians, these are food items in daily use. Finally, the invention of zero is often attributed to an ancient Indian mathematician, but it is also said that modern India has not learnt to move beyond zero.

Mustaches are a symbol of pride. Indian men adore them. In the state of Kerala, the majority of men have a mustache and if you find an odd one out, there is a very good chance he could be a migrant.

If the edges of the mustache are pointed upwards (tiger mustaches), they are a sign of an aggressive personality, tending to be royalty or just a bully. They apply body moisturizer to keep it pointing upwards. All the kings and conquerors of India have worn tiger mustaches. As part of body language, stroking a pointed mustache shows a higher sense of pride and people in rural areas treat it as a symbol of success. No wonder the man with longest moustache is an Indian. Mr. Ram Singh Chauhan has record-breaking 14ft moustache and his name is entered in the Guinness Book of World Records®.

Having to shave one's mustache is a most humbling experience and people are willing to lay down their lives rather than face public humiliation.

The sense of pride is at its peak whenever marriage is the topic. Inviting a guest does not end with presenting an invitation card. If the guest is very important, the invitation card has to be delivered in person by the parents along with gifts and sweets. The kind of gift will depend on the economic status of the host. Folded hands are a must whenever inviting a guest. Those guests who are important are invited in person along with the card. Other guests if outstation must be contacted with a special phone call, as well as the formal invitation. It is not asked if they would be able to come, instead it is insisted they must come.

Though hundreds of close relatives and friends of the family, all must be given an invitation card in person. Just sending the card by post and informing by e-mail is a definite recipe for relationship disaster. Doing so does mean that the invite is just for formality, the guest may not come. Long-standing close relationships that have lasted for decades, involving national personalities have been broken because of the failed diplomacy of the marriage invitation. An invitation to a marriage ceremony must accompany with ten strokes of pride to the guest.

An Indian living abroad adds few hundred points to his pride. Hence, on return to the country displays few characteristics to exhibit that newly added pride. They might have lived there for few months only, but when they return to India, their entire persona changes. Even a visit to a non-European country or the Americas for a couple of months will result in the acquisition of an American or British accent. In many cases, it is a mixture of both, or some strange accent that is neither, and certainly not an Indian. The moment they land at the airport, they start to complain about the weather being hot and that the place is too crowded, noisy and polluted. When expressing that frustration or any other, they take the opportunity to use American slang, which is understood by no one around. Everyone knows that this Indian has just been abroad. Drinking water is the next casualty, and they claim to prefer only the bottled water.

Honor and Respect:

Respect, or *Izzat* in Urdu and *Aadar Sammaan* in Hindi, is an important part of the culture which is ingrained into an Indian brain right from an early age. Anything which is personal is serious, especially when it comes to the following procedures in marriage, cooking, holding religious prayers or reciprocating respect.

Any object that is to do with knowledge and wisdom is not considered just a physical object, but an icon of the Goddess of Knowledge, *Swaraswati*. Children would never drop a book, a notebook or a pen on the floor or touch it with a foot. If they accidentally do, they would immediately lift it and seek an apology from the Goddess by kissing it and touching it to one's forehead. Children are more sensitive to this practice because they fear the Goddess, failing them in their exams.

Many things are viewed as auspicious and well-respected, such as the river Ganga. It is not considered just as a water body flowing from one direction to another. The Ganges should be called *Ganga Ji*, which is like being respectful to a holy mother. I was once traveling by train in India. When it was crossing over a long bridge, I asked my fellow passenger, out of geographical interest, if it was the river Ganga below. Immediately, he replied calling it *Ganga Mai*, (Mother Ganga) while holding his own ears in apology on my behalf, for calling her just by her name.

Similarly, teachers are highly respected and called *Gurus*, whose names are treated with great respect, holding one's own ears in apology for pronouncing their name. Teachers who teach music and other fine arts are also called *Guru*. They are highly respected and students honor them by touching their feet once before the start of the session. Students also revere their instruments like idols of God and any accidental instance of touching with the feet or harsh handling attracts sincere apologies and regret. They would also touch the floor of the stage then touch their forehead with the same hand, before their performance and before putting their feet on it. This gesture is to seek the blessings of the stage for a good performance.

For those Indians who are exposed to western pop culture, it is devastating, because bands perform while intoxicated and some of them smash their instruments after their performance.

Respect for money is another facet which an Indian can never lose sight of. In *Diwali*, the festival of light, the Goddess of wealth, *Laxmi*, is worshipped and so are the gold, silver and currency notes in the house. Even though throughout the year dirty money may change hands, it will find its place beside this powerful Goddess. Similar to school books, currency notes, coins and books of accounts are given the highest respect. For communities which are in business, their first and last act of every business day would be to offer prayers with incense sticks to the Goddess *Laxmi* and her symbols like the cash box and the accounts book. In shops, it is a usual scene that an early customer might have to wait patiently for a few minutes to let the prayers be completed. No one complains about that wait. The same is followed by Muslim, Christian or Indians of other religions too. Therefore, I think it is more to do with being an Indian.

Up to the very recent past, Indian companies were strangers to the concept of the 'pink slip' or 'getting fired'. It would be an extreme case of the company's bankruptcy or an employee's misconduct of the order of a crime that would attract that kind of action. Even though the Indian economy faced severe recession and sustained a meltdown in 2008, they have never laid off their employees. Those who did have foreign stakeholders, had to do it with a heavy heart. In return, their reputation took a beating. It is not that unions are not strong or vocal, but employers understand that primarily they support their employees' families. For the employees, working conditions may be tough and very demanding, but layoffs as seen in developed economies are a rarity.

Year after year, you will see the familiar faces of restaurant waiters, house maids and servants. They can last a lifetime with one employer. In their entire career, employees might change jobs only once or twice, with the exception of those in information technology. Many would not have had to write a resume in their entire career. This is not to mention government employees, who spend all of their work life there. India clearly sees a mutual respect and loyalty between the employers and employees, often to an extent of being slavish.

It is important to mention this, so that one knows that doing business in India is not just about business, but also about showing respect and commitment to a relationship. In business it is appropriate to address any senior person with 'Sir' and 'Ma'am', as calling someone by their first name is offensive. Even though western corporate etiquette encourages first-name culture, the Indian psyche is yet to accept that method. To play safe, one has to bestow as much respect as possible when addressing an Indian. White House's request for President Obama to address Indian Prime Minister as 'Manmohan' during his visit to India was declined by his office and "Dr. Singh" was suggested instead and accepted by the White House.

At schools, a teacher can complain to parents about their child's poor health and recommend a diet plan, a doctor can treat your elderly at home or even on the phone, college students may like to carry their professor's shopping bags, car mechanics can even suggest a fix for your two-wheeler and a hairdresser would not mind cutting a child's hair out of turn. It is all about respect for the relationship with the person concerned at that moment.

The best way to kill an Indian is not by shooting, but by disrespecting him. There are many simple and easy ways to do it.

Here are some:

- Don't offer him a seat, especially if elder to you
- Talk for long without offering tea or anything to eat
- Fail to invite him or his family to your wedding or birthday party
- Don't get up from your seat if he is your boss
- Call India a third world and poor country
- Put your feet up, even on a bed stool while talking
- Ask if he was killing flies, instead of working

- Refuse to eat what is offered, especially in festivals like Diwali, Eid or Christmas

- Prevent him to express a political opinion

- Ask him if he is a Pakistani

- Ask him if he is a Bangladeshi

- Address him as 'you' instead of his name with the respectful 'Ji' as a suffix (if he is older that you)

Fate:

Kismat or *Bhagya* is the Urdu and Hindi translations respectively. Every situation that is out of control is attributed to *Kismat*. Unlike the western outlook, where fate is not usually discussed in daily life, Indian *Kismat* is omnipresent, like God. Usually, it is combined with the wishes of the almighty. A good exam result is due to hard work and God's blessings, but failure is due either to *Kismat* or the wishes of the divine. Indians do not take personal responsibility for any failures, hence you will not hear 'it's my fault' or 'I should have seen it' or 'I erred' in any conversation.

Status:

Aukat or *Haisiyat* which are nearly the same as societal status make up for the personal positioning of every individual. This is the reference point for all communication and social transactions. India, being a highly hierarchical society, produces *Aukat* which, when combined with pride makes a lethal combination of arrogance and self-regard.

Since the society is status-centric, every Indian is judging themselves and others in order to gauge their status and the parity between the two. This makes Indians a community which is highly judgmental. They can judge the other on anything in a flip of a second.

Indians can judge by the way the other person dresses. The *saree* for the women has to be rightly placed around the neck, shoulder and waist. Usually wearing a jacket and a tie will immediately upgrade your status and elicit a positive response from the public. If you speak English, the social upgrade points can rise steeply with your fluency and vocabulary.

Indians are very judgmental about religion and caste, which can also define the future course of friendships and relationships. Many in India do not want to visit the west, just because they are beef and pork eating countries. Even in India, many Hindus would not accept anything from an Indian Muslim because they do eat beef.

Help:

Something which strikes me often in India is the propensity of Indians to help, especially strangers, either lost in the airports, stations or highways.

Also, it is worth mentioning that Indian roads do not have a very good system of showing directions. It is a usual practice by drivers to stop and shout at passers-by for directions. All of them oblige. Beware, some of them, just to protect their reputation of know-it-all, may give wrong information. Often, you will find them friendly and they may even leave their shop and customers to provide the information. Along with that, you can expect additional information like traffic conditions or the condition of the road itself. If that stranger happens to be going in that direction or the driver finds the route complicated, they will happily escort to the right place. When seeking that last mile direction in a village or a small town, there is a good chance that passers-by will know the addressee too. It happens very often. This is one more reason why GPS or Sat Nav is not really needed in India.

Sharm or Haya:

It is difficult to define the exact English translation. *Sharm* in Hindi and *Haya* in Urdu are composite guidelines for being a Good Samaritan. Even though they are broad guidelines, they can be cited as rules. In the practice people's social conduct is based on the *Sharm* or *Haya*. Many of the guidelines cover areas of etiquettes, dressing sense, tone of conversation, usage of words and conflict management.

Indians live in a widely accepted contradictory society and therefore, the concept of Sharm and Haya is loosely used, mostly to one's own convenience. The conduct of women in public is the most sought after reference to these guidelines. Their dressing is the first point of judgment which can raise passionate and high voltage discussions. It usually lands Indians in a conflict with women liberty versus traditionalism.

Like many other topics, Indians are most confused with this one. For example, while Sharm or Haya seeks to restrain the public display of bodies, the cities are lined up with billboards of exposing models of Indian and foreign origin. It is a growing trend and extensively used to advertise fancy products and movies. In films, most popular are the actresses who can bare it all, of course along with their acting skills. While pelvic movements in dances are very popular on screens, the action is not appreciated if done in the family gathering.

Over the period, this fundamental philosophy has become more of a guideline for women. Obviously, the Indian brides, especially the new ones come under intense scrutiny. Their conduct is under a social microscope for wearing the veil, touching the feet of elders, greeting protocols, ornaments, dressing sense – both formal and informal, general etiquettes and may others. Boys and men easily get away from the judgment and are less penalized for their infringement.

Karma and Seven Lives:

Oh yes. The existence of seven lives is where the belief in *karma* comes from. It is not one single life that has to be worried about; Indians have seven such lives according to this fundamental Indian mythological belief. Even though science has not proved it (yet), it does not make it unreal. So the *karma* (act) that one does in this birth, good or bad, will receive reward or punishment in this lifetime or in any of the forthcoming six lives. Indians do not consider that a few of those seven lives may already have been lived. The existence of seven lives is supposed to prevent people from doing bad *karma*. What goes around comes around of essence which will happen any time within the next seven lives. So why spoil future with a mistake in this life?

It is the same reasoning that applies when one suffers with pain, agony, losses, separations, failures, etc. It is said that one is paying for the bad *karma* from a past life. In a way it is also a ray of hope for no more suffering in the next life.

> **Goods things in this life,**
> **is reward of good karma in previous life.**
> **Vice-versa.**

For some reason, if pain and sufferings are unbearable in this life, Indians conduct special prayer services on auspicious days to clean up the previous *karma* records. Taking a holy dip in river Ganges (*Ganga Mai*) is one of the serious recommendations. Also, millions like to be cremated on the banks of holy Ganges or their ashes immersed, to surmount the effects of bad *karma* and get relieved for a better rebirth.

Q

- Quotient of Colors

Quotient of Colors

Indians use many lively and stimulating colors, very bright ones not only in their dress, but wherever possible in their daily lifestyle. Starting from the *sarees* and other women's dresses, the fabrics are made in all the shades of the rainbow and more. Men also wear dazzling colors in their shirts and sweaters. Watching men wearing turbans, the brightness is often glaring. Walking past the rural markets is a treat, to see the radiance of the culture.

The walls of the homes have vivid paints and often the walls of the same room can have multiple colors. The doors are vibrant with primary colors and so also the door frames are decorated.

The roads are filled densely with multicolored trucks and pickup vehicles. There are special paint shops and artists who do exclusive artwork and decoration to the truck's exterior. They are painted with lively pictures of Gods and Goddesses, Bollywood stars, spiritual quotations and words of wisdom. No one can miss these drivers. They blow high-pitched horns at the same time as if to flash their joyous loud colors.

Red is the insignia of brides and a happy marriage. Festivals, also an emblem of happiness, erupt majestically with extraordinary colors. It attracts all the shades in all seasons. India is also a place for a colossal festival of colors called *Holi*. All across India, millions throw colors at each other while wishing them the best of times ahead. In a two-day festival, the streets are filled with Indians of all ages, dressed in clothes that culminate into palate. These dresses don't go for a wash but rather given away or thrown away. Indians require one hard scrubbing to remove all the color from the body.

Like the Indian dressing, the Indian Gods and Goddess are also dressed and decorated in striking colors. Richer the temple, magnificent is the costume and décor. From flowers to ornaments, wall paintings to lighting, offerings of spiritual gifts, all are composed of loudness of colors, glitter and sound.

So splendid is the use of hue and luminosity of Indians that sometimes it is difficult to differentiate if all days are festivals or festivals happen every day.

R

- Relatives and Relationships
    - List of named relationships
    - Rakhi and Bhai Dooj
    - Karvachauth
- Religions
- Restaurants
- Reaching India
- Roadside Assistance

Relatives and Relationships

Indian society, hierarchical by caste, is also sliced and diced by one's relationships within the family and extended family. A family, in terms of daily interactions, does not stop at just the husband, wife and children, but extends in a long chain of members on both the maternal and the paternal side. The maternal and paternal uncles, their aunts, their children, the maternal uncles' and aunts' spouses, their in-laws and their children have a special place in the household dynamics. Each relationship has a name so it is not as generic as just 'uncles' and 'aunts'. Each member is addressed by their relationship to that person. The interesting part is the permutations and combinations, one has to remember, to establish the identity of a person, as each member has a different name for that relationship. While each calls each other by a different designation, still everyone else knows who is being talked about. Since it becomes complicated, the first name along with the relationship name is used. This provides both: the identity as well as respect. Using just the name would be a relationship-breaker.

Brides, especially newlyweds, have a special task ahead of them. They have to learn about all the important people in the relationship as quickly as possible. This is because she is judged by her response to the elderly and towards young ones. She is required to be extremely respectful to anybody older than herself, and to be very loving to younger ones. Everyone as well as the husband has to approve of her conduct and charm. Since India is a joint family system, the new bride has an uphill task of managing relationships and marketing herself as the best daughter-in-law, called *Bahu*. The challenging task has become even more demanding as popular soap operas portray daughters-in-law with very high standards. With the best intentions, it would require no less than a superhuman effort to achieve this. This leaves the real-world brides in the shadow of those on the silver screen, desperate for more opportunities that test their mettle. For a bride, managing relationships with the in-laws and their extended family is a complex feat of juggling. The complexity grows with the age of the in-laws. The importance and priority that must be given by the bride to these members exponentially increase with age. Senior ladies seek more compliance, as they keep a sharp eye on observing, instructing, correcting and directing the right ways (they think) of doing things.

List of named relationships:

Paternal Grand Father	Paternal Grand Mother	Maternal Grand Father	Maternal Grand Mother
Dada	Dadi	Dada	Dadi
Father	**Father's Elder Brother**	**Father's Elder Brother's Wife**	
Papa	Tao	Tai	
Father's Younger Brother	**Father's Younger Brother's Wife**		
Chacha	Chachi		
Father's Sister	**Father's Sister's Husband**		
Bua	FooFa		

Mother	Mother's Brother	Mother's Brother's Wife
Ma	Mama	Mami

Elder Brother	Elder Brother's Wife	Younger Brother	Younger Brother's Wife
Bhaiya	Bhabhi	Bhaiya	Bhabhi
	Equivalent to Status of Mother		
Brother's Son	**Brother's Daughter**		
Bhatija	Bhatiji		

Elder Sister	Younger Sister	Sister's Husband
Didi	Behan	Jija
Sister's Son	**Sister's Son's Wife**	
Bhanja	Bhanja Bahu	
Sister's Daughter	**Sister's Daughter's Husband**	
Bhanji	Jamai	

Son	Daughter
Beta	Beti
Son's Wife	**Daughter's Husband**
Bahu	Jamai
Grandson	**Granddaughter**
Pota	Poti

If one were to make a chart for the family in order of important people, those perched on the top would are the ones who are most aged. Their opinion will be sought on all important issues, including jobs, marriage, pregnancy, health and general family dynamics. This is to leverage the wisdom from their experience.

Since each relationship has a name, people in a family are addressed by that name. This would be the most respectful way. In case you come across a person who is not known to you, you also have ways to address them respectfully, which could be a situation that occurs in a very large gathering of friends and family.

Any elderly male can be addressed as *chacha* or father's younger brother, and a very elderly male can be called *dada*, or grandfather. If the lady is of the same age group as one's mother, she is called *chachi*, or father's younger brother's wife, and if the lady is very old, elderly enough to use a walking stick, she may be addressed as *mataji* or grandmother. People of similar ages are called *bhai saab* or big brother. Ladies of the same age as yours can be addressed as *behenji* or elder sister. If you think a woman might take offense by attaching an age factor in calling her *behenji*, the Indian system provides the option of calling these age-conscious ladies *bhabhi* or brother's wife. This nomenclature is valid for all the strangers one meets, not only in a gathering of blood relatives, but also on the street, and in shops, restaurants and other places. In the state of Gujarat, all women, irrespective of their age, are addressed as sisters or *bhen*.

Rakhi

The brother-sister relationship is a fundamental defining one in Indian society. India holds a very important festival called *Rakhi*, which is meant especially for brothers and sisters to show their mutual commitment. In India's violent history, invaders to a kingdom made women vulnerable to brutality. Hence, their brothers were assigned the religious duty of protecting their sisters, even if they have to sacrifice their own lives. The tradition is followed today, and brothers are committed to looking after their sisters. Brothers will travel great distances and often undertake overseas journeys to be with their sisters on this special day. The festive pitch is similar to what is seen during 'Thanks Giving' in the US.

The sister ties a protective band, a symbol binding the brother to his divine duty. This relationship is taken very seriously, to be honored until the end of life. The festival is celebrated across all religions in India, making it a truly 'Indian' festival. The concept can apply not just to real brothers, but also to cousins.

Some other relationships are also essentially Indian. For example, there is the idea of *Rakhi Brothers*. This has significant abilities to bind two strangers into a relationship. It can also be an emotional bonding of a girl considering a boy in the neighborhood to be her brother. She can offer to tie the protective band to demonstrate their relationship.

The commitment is demanding. The brother and the *Rakhi Brother* take an automatic father-like responsibility for supporting the sister, even though he can be much younger. It is an honorable duty that a brother from India will have to perform. Nowhere else in the world, is this relationship given such an esteemed status.

Karvachauth

As in any other part of the world, husbands have a special place in a woman's life. It is more so in India because they are often the primary breadwinners. As a society, a woman's status without a husband has no meaning, even if she commands endless wealth and fame. Though it may be viewed negatively as male-dominated, it is seen as acceptable because country's history has developed that way.

India has been invaded by many since time immemorial. War makes women vulnerable and subject to all kinds of abuse. In earlier centuries, if a husband died for reasons of war, accident or ill health, the wife was left unprotected to face the world's brutality. In order to prevent this, the woman committed something termed 'glorious suicide', or *Sati*. Sadly, it was the custom in those days. The woman, fearing a painful end, started to worship the moon God to help secure her husband's life. Thankfully, the practice of *Sati* has come to an end, but the best practice of worshipping the moon continues to this day.

On the special day of *Karvachauth*, which is the full moon day of autumn, the wife holds a day-long abstinence from food and water, to please the moon God. They break their fast after sighting the full moon and offering prayers. This is a very special day in a married woman's life.

Even in this modern hectic life, an Indian husband makes every effort to be with his wife on this day. All travel away from home is avoided.

The womenfolk are dressed in the best of their bridal wear, irrespective of their age. It is a mix of romantic and religious fervor, with prayers and rituals. The brightness of the full moon adds to the festivities with their bright colors and candle light.

Suddenly, Indian men can start looking selfish. Men folk don't want their wives to break that fast without observing the full moon and prayers. It could be an impediment to them. So they all want their wives to commit to *Karvachauth*. Hence, they do their best, throughout the day, to comfort their hungry wife.

Religions

Religion is of high priority in India. Still higher priority is the rigor in observing the version of their religion which people practice. The number of variations in a religion can be as many as the number of streets in a neighborhood. This means that most of the population follows their own version of Hinduism. There are no specific names for these versions, but the differences lie in following a particular belief, observing a fast, different ways of celebrating festivals, unique rituals, vegetarianism and non-vegetarianism, and worshipping their favorite God. Even though a person can be non-vegetarian, during certain periods of the year or week complete vegetarianism will be observed. Though it might not be religious, some Indians prefer to be vegetarian when one in the family is pregnant.

Indians strongly believe in reincarnation, and that the comfort of the next life is based on good karma in the current life. This gives Indians a powerful reason behind any event in their current lifetime. If the event produces happiness and joy, it is attributed to some good work in a previous life and vice versa. As Indians grow older, this consideration of karma becomes more constant. An elderly Indian is highly religious and devotes more and more time in pursuit of spirituality, to clear away the sins in their current life and receive a better life in the next.

These are a few concepts that are not seen in any other major religions of the world. Observing a fast is considered not only about not eating food during the day, it is also about controlling hunger and conditioning the brain. Islam also preaches fasting in the holy month of *Ramzan*.

For Hindus, all seven days of the week define fasting for different Gods and prayers for the fulfillment of a particular kind of wish. Observing a fast on a particular day of the week would mean pleasing a particular God for a specific purpose.

List of Hindu Gods and dedicated fasting days:

Days of Worship	Name of God / Goddess	Code for Fasting	Offering
SUNDAY	Lord Surya (Sun God)	Eat only Once a day Oil and Salt is avoided	Red Flower
MONDAY	Lord Shiva	Sunrise to Sunset	White Flower Bel Patra
TUESDAY	Lord Ganesha	Avoid taking salt in dinner Single meal of wheat and jaggery	Red Flower
	Goddess Durga		
	Goddess Kali		
	Lord Hanuman		
WEDNESDAY	Lord Vithal (Incarnation of Lord Krishna)	24 hour fasting with one afternoon meal	Tulsi Leaves (Holy Basil)
THURSDAY	Lord Vishnu	Once a day meal of milk product and Yellow lentils	Milk and Ghee (Butter Oil) Yellow Flower and Fruits
FRIDAY	Mother Goddess Durga	Sunrise to Sunset	White coloured Food Kheer (Rice Pudding)

A-Z Dealing with Indians

SATURDAY	Lord Shani Lord Hanuman to protect from wrath of Lord Shani	Single meal in the evening after prayers Food prepared in Sesame oil Food items colored Black	Black Grams Sesame Oil Black Sesame Black Cloth

It is said that in the Hindu religion, there are as many as 330 million Gods and Goddess. Each one is capable of fulfilling a particular type of wish of mortals. For example, one God could bless the devotee with wealth and fame, another one could bless with a loving husband. A loving husband is a life's mission for millions of Indian women. Another powerful God can keep your family safe from all evils.

Deities can be in the form of a particular tree, animal, mountain, bird, reptile, human, or even a fish. It is interesting to note that girls before puberty are also considered as deities. They are worshipped as a symbol of the Goddess *Durga* during the festival of *Navratra*, in the month of October.

Name of God / Goddess	Planet God	Effect
Lord Surya (Sun God)	Sun God	Fulfilling Desires
Lord Shiva	Moon God	Unmarried women get ideal husband Others get good married life
Lord Ganesha	Mars God	Overcoming difficulties in life Couples planning to have son
Goddess Durga	Mars God	
Goddess Kali	Mars God	
Lord Hanuman	Mars God	
Lord Vithal	Mercury God	Auspicious day to start new business
Lord Vishnu	Jupiter God	Wealth and Happy Life
Mother Goddess Durga	Venus God	Removal of Obstacles Material wealth
Lord Shani Lord Hanuman to protect from wrath of Lord Shani	Saturn God	Protection from wrath of Lord Shani

The Gods and Goddesses are also patronized by different states of India. While people can follow any religion, Gods or Goddesses, each state has a favorite deity. This also means that on the occasion assigned to that deity, it is a state holiday.

Indian states and their most followed Hindu Gods:

Jammu and Kashmir – Lord Shiva

Punjab – Sikh Gurus

Bihar – Lord Krishna

Uttar Pradesh – Lord Ram Chandra and Lord Krishna

Bengal – Goddess Durga, Goddess Kali Mata

Gujarat – Lord Krishna

Maharastra – Lord Ganesh

Goa – St. Xavier

Andhra Pradesh – Lord Tirupati Balaji

Tamil Nadu – Lord Tirupati Balaji

In general, religions in India are also linked to colors. It is white and silver for Christians, olive green for Muslims, saffron for Hindus and yellow for Sikhs. But if it is red, they are communists. Certainly, these colors are not to be confused with the colors adopted by political parties.

Many times, one can see a male Indian colleague with a red or white mark between the eyebrows. You might wonder about the purpose of this colored spot. It is a water-based paste of lead oxide and sandalwood, which an Indian applies on the forehead, every morning after their worship. It is a belief that this spot keeps them protected from all evils throughout the day. This makes worshipping every morning as compulsory an action as breathing. If the start of the day is set aside for prayer service, it is also necessary to take a shower or bath as a sign of purity.

Most Hindus worship twice a day, once in the morning and one towards the end of the day. This makes bathing an important feature of the daily routine. Similarly, Muslims hold prayers five times a day and they either bathe or take a religious wash before the sacred act. It makes religion responsible for making Indians almost obsessive-compulsive bathers.

Bathing in India means pouring water over oneself using a mug, drawn from a bucket. Unlike the west, most Indian bathrooms have only this bucket-mug system. Not because it is a habit, but rather that running water is a rarity. Since the water supply in the taps is not continuous in India, people have to store water in buckets and drums. It is one issue which all Indian households have to worry about throughout their life. Now a day, the showers are common in bathrooms, but still you can spot a bucket and mug in the very same bathroom. One can limit the use of water using the bucket but not with shower.

Religion is so much part of life that there is no celebration without a prayer service. Religion comes into an Indian life more often than one could expect. It is engrained in every moment and is followed with utmost sincerity. Whether it is charity work, routine business or committing a crime, the participants follow their religious rituals. Here are just some examples, because the list could be a book in itself. A full ceremony to worship and thank God is held when a child is born, graduation, when a new car is bought or a new home is purchased, when getting engaged and married, when starting a journey, before going for an exam and when excelling in any result, academic or business. These are all special occasions. Whatever happens as special events, daily prayer is separate.

If the occasion is special and exceptional, Indians perform *havan*. It is a prayer service with chanting of scriptures and offerings like grain (wheat or rice), butter-oil (*ghee*), fruits and other items in a consecrated fire. These occasions could be a marriage, a new home, rains; India wins the Cricket World Cup, a politician getting bailed from jail, bringing peace to a departed soul, and much more. It is the usual practice to commit to a *havan*, so that a wish comes true. This kind of prayer service is a public service where family, friends and neighbors can participate.

A common kind of get together, called 'katha' or 'Paath' or 'kirtan' is where friends, family and neighbors are invited for recitation of a holy book or holy songs with some snacks or lunch afterwards. The recitation could be carried out by a priest and friends and family would also participate for a part of it. Such events could be triggered by good news in the family like a new baby being born, a child topping his exam, a wedding or even without any such occasions.

There is a separate place of worship in every house, office, restaurant, shop and place of work. If Indians cannot find a place to put a picture of their God, they keep one in their wallet or display it as wallpaper on their laptop.

Gods' idols and pictures are the most decorated and ornate space in the establishment. There are pearls, glitter, plenty of fresh flowers, fragrance, incense sticks and fresh fruits. If people are not able to create an exotic space for their Gods, they keep a well-decorated picture. It is no surprise that children have a picture of their favorite God in their pencil box. Even an automobile's dashboard has a place for the divinity. Many enthusiasts fill up their entire rear windscreen with the almighty's stickers, blessing the vehicle from any untoward incident. Mobile phones and their covers are no strangers to God's presence either.

Every year, in the month of October, thousands of temporary stages are set up across India and abroad to perform scenes from the great Indian mythology *Ramayan*. The actors impersonate the Gods and demons with very high spirits and religious compliance. It is interesting to find that all the characters, before undertaking the role, go through a process of self-purification. They do not consume alcohol or non-vegetarian food during a period of those seven days. Also, they sleep on the floor like the sages, because during those seven days of staging mythology, the audience treats them as impersonations of a God itself. People hold prayer services in which the 'humans' playing the role of a

God or Goddess are worshipped as if the divinities have set foot on earth.

For the benefit of those who are new to Indian culture, *Ramayan* is one of the two great Indian epics and the longest in the world. The other Hindu epic is called *Mahabharat*. It has 24,000 verses and 500 cantos. Since, it is the core of Hindu literature, it is also treated as the history of Hinduism.

Although verses and stories from the *Ramayan* and *Mahabarat* are taught in schools, parents and grandparents use episodes from the two epics as bedtime stories. It is primarily to build a child's character and make them God fearing. Hence, every Indian knows the storyline by heart, still they find time in this festive season to enjoy the mythological play. The play is conducted by both professionals and assorted talent from the neighborhood, depending on the budget of the local association.

In an Indian movie, the first thing that is displayed after the censorship board's certificate is a picture of God. For those in small business, every day, before the start of the first business transaction, prayers are offered. It is only after this ritual that business is assumed to be open for the day. The same happens at the end of the business day. After the last transaction has been completed, prayers are offered. Unlike western terminology of declaring a business closed for the day, in India it is said that 'the business has prospered to the next day'. Referring to one's shop or business as 'closed' is considered derogatory or unlucky. "Closed" means "Closed Down". There is no notice board carrying the word "Closed" on it. If the shop or store has closed for the day, it is indicated by the pulled down shutter. Certainly, an owner would never call his establishment 'closed', in order to prevent any bad omen affecting prosperity.

Commitment to God is surprisingly very high compared with what we do in the west. Although it is a mix of being ritualistically religious and superstitious, still it is notable that India as a civilization has no limitations. Anybody can follow any religion unless they are hampering the peace of society.

The consequence of having so many religions in India makes it a very philosophical society. Anyone can start a discussion about spirituality. Everyone knows the supreme God as if He himself has passed on the messages to them. This chapter might never end, and volumes can be written about religions in India. Hence a good and logical conclusion would be to say that each Indian is very different from the other. Beliefs can be very diverse, and even contradictory between two individuals. There is no one formula to define the religious practices followed, even though they all belong to the four major religions of the world.

Be surprised, if you are not surprised!

Restaurants

Restaurant culture is not only about authentic food but also about the courteous way it is served. It has little to do with socializing and meeting friends for a long chit-chat.

When a guest arrives at the table, the response of the waiter defines the class of the restaurant. If the server does not hand out a menu, instead recites the entire menu of nearly forty dishes in one breathe, it is a high probability that you are sitting in a roadside inexpensive restaurant called 'dhabha'. I can guarantee the excellent taste of the upcoming dishes, though in a basic rustic setting. As you place the order, the waiter shouts to cook from that table itself to prepare the order for this particular guest. It is not this waiter but the assistant waiter who would serve the right dish to the right guest which will leave you wondering about the best practices of in-house communication. Though the server seems to be in a hurry, they would never miss any detail of your order. While it is an amazement to hear out the menu recital, it is also a delight to see this hi-tech paperless ordering system working falwlessly.

In a next level of restaurant, the waiter might just hand out a menu, which will be no more than a laminated two A4 page list and he might not wait for your order. In case, he does so, there is a good chance, he is also attending partially to the next table or passing instructions to his colleagues in words or gestures. This is while you are trying to understand the dishes as they do not have an explanation on the menu. It is assumed in all restaurants that a guest knows the ingredients of the dish. Mostly the dishes are generic and if not, the name itself would suggest the ingredients. Subsequently, if you need additional cutlery, it will come straight from the waiter's shirt pocket and handed over to you after a brief wipe with his cloth napkin. This is a middle class restaurant, trying to graduate to a posher level.

If the restaurant is not posh, it might be possible to just walk in and find an empty table, and not wait for someone to assign a table to you.

If the waiter comes with a notepad, hand out a leather covered menu book to each of the guests and waits patiently to take the order, one can be assured to be in a posh restaurant. The waiter will communicate with a soft voice and will be very courteous. Probably the payments can be made with a card and a tip is expected.

The definition of good service is rated by the timeliness of the food arriving at the table, the number of times the server came to check the dishes. Not to mention that the food's taste has to be close to your mother's home-cooked food. The server not only has to keep the food on the table, but to serve it on your plate, even for multiple servings.

In western culture, the host's responsibility for serving the food is often defined up to the time the food is placed on the table. In Indian culture, serving the food goes a step further by putting the food on the guest's plate. It is at this step that the core of Indian hospitality rests, and that defines the level of honor bestowed upon the guest. For Indians, especially at home, serving food also involves requesting the guests to eat. If any of these steps is missed, the guest might not be pleased enough to sustain the relationship. At home, if hosts want to show extra respect and love, it is better to ask people to eat multiple times. If your relationship is on the informal side, the host would even push you to have more. In a situation where the guest indicates a liking for a particular dish, it becomes the host's responsibility to gently insist on having multiple servings.

There is a very predictable sequence of steps that happen in a typical restaurant. On arriving at the table, you are served with water while still settling in your place. Orders are sought within the next few minutes. Once served on your plates by the server, you are served again by the waiter somewhere in the middle of your meal. When you have finished, it is a good thing to assess the food with a few burps. A burp means the guest has enjoyed the food and therefore the belly is full up to the brim. Since everyone eats with their hands, once finished a bowl is provided on the table with warm water and a slice of lemon. Now you should know that this warm water is not to drink. Lemon in hot water works well to ease out the oil on the hands and helps clean nicely. The bill is produced by the waiter, and it must be accompanied by fennel seeds, otherwise it is considered rude. The fennel seeds are also called 'mouth fresheners'. They are a polite indicator that the welcome has come to a conclusion. Toothpicks are also served along with the mouth fresheners and guests can be seen sticking one into their wisdom teeth while making payment. The place is left quickly after paying.

Usually restaurants are very busy and therefore the expectation even from the restaurant owners is that you quickly order, eat a lot and leave as soon as possible. Do not be surprised if you get the bill (check) while you are still finishing your dessert. Unlike restaurants in the west, where you might like to go slowly, hang out with your company, sip coffee or tea, read a book or work on your laptop, most Indian restaurants are very fast-paced. A waiter might even ask you to leave, in order to make space for the next guests. So restaurants in India are just a place to eat. If you really want to hang out, that happens either at roadside tea shops or the very fancy ones in the five-star hotels. By the way, restaurants in India are also called hotels in common parlance.

Tipping is not mandatory, especially if they are not the rated restaurants. As a habit, Indians don't tip though may learn to do so at some point in time. Good reason for not tipping is exactly not known. At best one can guess that Indians do not find the extra economic value in the labor and service. According to them, tips are for the server who had just brought the dishes while the real work was done by the cook.

The next stop is the *pan* shop which is a necessity, though a separate entity, from the restaurant. The *pan* shop is a kiosk which is no bigger than a few square feet, usually run by a single person. He sits with folded legs and prepares a customized and on-demand *pan* for all his customers. A *pan* is a fresh betel leaf folded and stuffed with compulsory items like paste of acacia catechu bark and lime, and optional fillings like a pinch of *gulqand* (a sweet paste of rose petal), crushed Areca nuts, ground coconut flakes, cardamom, cloves, tobacco of different strengths, and fennel seeds. Since the betel leaf bulges out with overflowing stuffing, it is manually stapled with a couple of clove sticks and presented to the customer. The *pan* chef also supplies loose cigarettes, which usually go along with the *pan*. The *pan* shop is a place with no hurry, unlike the restaurant. Indians like to eat *pan*, chew tobacco and/or smoke one while standing at the front of the *pan* shop. It has a characteristic jute rope hanging, with a perpetually smoldering fire for the convenience of smokers to light their cigarette. Over a period of time, the *pan* chef becomes acquainted with the taste and preferences of their repeat customers. Hence, reordering would not mean re-specification of the *pan*. It is an honor for an Indian to patronize a *pan* shop where he gets a personalized *pan* without even mentioning any preferences. Often these shops are also a place to hang out, gossip and discuss the seasonal topics of politics, movies, sports or other sensational news. The *pan* chef is usually part of the conversation, and if not, certainly overhears the discussions. In that sense, the chef is highly informed and knowledgeable about global, national and local topics. For sociologists and surveillance, the *pan* chef is a goldmine of intelligence.

Eating a mouthful of *pan* is unlike any other food in the world. Technically, eating a *pan* is like chewing a never-ending lollipop. It can sit there on one side of the mouth for hours, filling it with juice, slowly. It does not hamper the routine of an Indian, rather it *is* the routine. Indians chew and then spit the juice all over. *Pan* spit is more than the conventional spit and less than a fire hose.

How do you know when a person is going to spit? If an Indian is talking with his head up, and it gets higher and higher, his voice becomes blurred with every syllable and his lips close in a perfect circle, it is time to get away, because the spit hose is imminent. Expert *pan* eaters can direct their spit hose accurately to a particular corner of public buildings. It is a no-brainer to find spots with the scribble of *pan* spits across the country's public places.

> **However, satisfied your appetite is, there is always room for *pan*.**

The *pan* shop is part of the Indian culture, as is the pub culture of the west. These shops line up along Indian roads. Over a period of time, they have become a center of convenience and a source of emergency household provisions. They have bread, butter, eggs, chocolates, mobile charge cards, packaged snacks, a public telephone, milk, Coke, Pepsi and other soft drinks. Most importantly, they are the classical Indian GPS. If an Indian is lost, a *pan* shop is always there to give directions. It is the most used service after the *pan* itself.

However, crowded a bus is, there is always room for the driver. The same could be said about *pan*. However, satisfied your appetite is, there is always room for *pan*.

Reaching India

India is a land of colors, aromas, noise, chaos and an ocean of humanity. As soon as you are out of the airport, people will be soliciting for different services. Someone would like to push your cart, another might offer to carry your baggage, and numerous taxi drivers will seek your attention. There will also be crowds of onlookers, observing your reaction to these exchanges. Especially if you do not look like a person of South Asian descent, then start feeling like a celebrity. People around will give extended looks and would attempt to engage with you.

India is very well connected with other parts of the world and there are numerous flights to get into India. Those are official ways. The citizens of neighboring countries like Bangladesh and Nepal can walk-in across their farms and many daring ones from Sri Lanka take boat to India when in distress.

India is a very welcoming country for both legal and illegal immigrants. Cities like Mumbai and Delhi are full of both. It is so welcoming that there exists no official count of the illegal migration and I doubt if there is any ready figure for the legal ones too.

Reaching India requires a visa and formal application via the respective Indian consulate and embassies. There have been many cases where American citizens have crossed the seven seas to reach India after a grueling eighteen to twenty hours, only to be deported. Their assumption of travelling to India without visa like they did in Europe and Canada fell flat. Hence it is advised to refer to the official government of India website for the visa requirements or refer to this book.

Roadside Assistance

Roadside assistance is not just limited to fixing the broken automobiles. India can boast of having roadside assistance for nearly everything possible. In a way, it can also be said that the majority of Indians and Indians business live and thrive on the road side. India is a country of narrow roads with shops and businesses spilling onto the road network. Even if it is a national highway, except for the few express motorways, shops line up along the sides of the roads. As one arrives at the towns and cities, the congestion and roadside bustle increases exponentially. In many places, a mix of formal shops, roadside kiosks, traveling salesmen along with shoppers and their vehicles cover the roads with sea of Indian humanity. In this mix, one can find roadside assistance, very cheap, for all those things which might be formal, expensive and difficult to find in other parts of the world.

- Ear wax cleaning
- Tarot reading by parrots
- Palmistry and astrology
- Knife and scissor sharpening
- Bicycle repair
- Tire puncture repair
- Laundry services
- Steel and Iron works, including welding

- Two-wheeler repair
- Pirated music and movie CDs
- Second-hand books and magazines
- Shoeshine and shoe repairs
- Umbrella repair
- Zip repair
- Men's hair cutting and shaving
- Teeth cleaning
- Bone fracture repair (rural areas)

S

- Spiritual Chanting and Home Temples
- Schools
- Safety is for Dumb, to Secure is Smartness

Spiritual Chanting and Home Temples

The major religions in India, both Hindus and Muslims, have a practice of spiritual chanting. While Muslims have a schedule of having prayers five times a day, Hindus can undertake chanting at any time of the day. As mentioned before, chanting is conditional on taking baths, which is a necessary part of carrying out any religious activity. All Indian families irrespective of their religion start their day only after taking a bath and offering prayer at home. On the way to work, if there is a place of worship, they also like to attend in person or make a respectable bow when driving by it. An Indian living in any other country will follow the same habit, even though the weather or work schedule may add to the inconvenience.

Spiritual chanting is the best insurance.

One might wonder about the uniqueness of chanting. Auspicious chanting numbers of Hindus are 11, 21, 51, 108 and 1008. The most suitable number of the common man is 108, which is not too much to disturb the daily routine, nor too little to miss the attention of their favorite God. Hindu scriptures are rhymes which are dedicated to the time of day, the purpose of the chanting, and the God to whom it is dedicated. It is understood that there are some 330 million Gods and Goddesses, but most worship only a few of them. People can choose which they want to patronize and pick the scriptures they want to devote while chanting.

The chanting is done with a rosary, the same way as it is done across all religions and countries in the world. It is made from the stem of the plant called 'Holy Basil' or a special tree called *Rudraksh or* Blueberry Bead, which grows only in the Himalayas. It is understood that the natural frequency of the Blueberry Bead, as defined by the laws of physics, is same as the human heart, therefore considered good for its function. It needs to be verified, as it is only a claim. Many Hindus also wear it around their neck while they are awake.

When a particular religion has many Gods to choose from, it results in a typical behavior which is found only in Hinduism. They have the luxury of picking and choosing their devotions. Alignment to a favorite God depends on that deity's power as depicted in mythology. The association to a particular God is also influenced by the family. A Hindu family is identified with the God whom they follow as a family tradition. It also depends on the kind of insurance and comprehensive coverage provided by devotion to a particular God.

List of Hindu Gods and their effects on devotees:

Name of God / Goddess	Planet God	Effect
Lord Surya (Sun God)	Sun God	Fulfilling Desires
Lord Shiva	Moon God	Unmarried women to get ideal husband. Others get good married life
Lord Ganesha	Mars God	Overcoming difficulties in life Couples planning to have son
Goddess Durga	Mars God	
Goddess Kali	Mars God	
Lord Hanuman	Mars God	
Lord Vithal	Mercury God	Auspicious day to start new business
Lord Vishnu	Jupiter God	Wealth and Happy Life
Mother Goddess Durga	Venus God	Removal of Obstacles Material wealth
Lord Shani / Lord Hanuman to protect from	Saturn God	Protection from wrath of Lord Shani

All Indian homes necessarily have a small temple. If you walk into an Indian's home, even those homes which are outside India, you will find a picture of God, a religious corner and an idol. It is usual to find pictures of various Gods in the living room too.

For Hindus, mostly the home temple is in the kitchen or a separate prayer room, facing the north or east corner of the house. For Muslims, it has to face towards Holy Mecca. Footwear is not allowed in and around those places.

Although Gods are omnipresent, it is Indians who have made them visible everywhere. The places where images of a God can be found as a constant reminder of his presence are automobile dashboards, mobile phone backgrounds, computer screen savers, wallets, doors, the top of visiting cards, one corner of a shop's name plate, letterheads, calendars, gift boxes, personal diary, children's notebooks and places of work and study. It is said sarcastically, that only **God knows how things work in India**.

A peculiar trend in mobile communication which is found in India is the spiritual 'caller tune'. In the west, if someone calls a landline or mobile, it is the classic ringing tone that is heard before the response. If you call an Indian friend's mobile, it is likely that you would hear spiritual chanting or a Bollywood song instead of that classic ring. Even though it is a paid service, still Indians opt for it in order to ward off any bad omens or unpleasant news coming through the phone call.

Chanting can also be heard aloud as a mobile ringtone. Imagine yourself in a serious official meeting or a thriller movie and suddenly spiritual chanting goes off. Indians think they need a perpetual reminder of God's presence, everywhere. There was a time when cars played spiritual chanting whenever a reverse gear was applied. Not only did it alert the bystanders of the reversing vehicle, but it sounded the arrival of one's devotion in the neighborhood. Although I haven't seen this practice for a long time.

Schools

An average Indian school will have a few thousand children. In big cities, space constrains them to hold classes like an industrial system. In the same building, school runs in shifts. The primary and secondary class students arrive at different times of the day. The effect of the rising Indian population is visible in the schools and classrooms too. The average class size is sixty children, all crammed around tables in twos and threes. By the time the class teacher starts to recognize the faces, their annual session is already over.

You will find children carrying heavy school bags, at times heavier than their own weight. There is a huge amount of homework given, to be completed for the next day. In effect, children have their curriculum divided between school and home. Homework engages parents too, and is probably more stressful for the parents than for the children. No wonder India is producing so many qualified professionals, as schools and homes have become a hothouse for educated brains.

> **Every year, no other country, churns more English speaking population, than India does.**

School culture is very different from the real world. Teachers hold a very special place when it comes to showing respect. Unlike in western countries, where children view teachers as government workers or care personnel, in India they are placed on a very high pedestal, with elements of gratitude and reverence. This makes the administration of discipline in the school very different from the conventions of western civilization. Teachers often whip children, of course with sensitivity. The parents allow this and at times recommend that teachers handle their child's discipline issues. It can scare children into being better-behaved both at school and at home. If parents observe any 'incorrect' habit or behavior in their child, they would share it with teachers and ask for their help in correcting the same.

Other forms of disciplining at school include standing on the bench and holding one's ears, kneeling down in front of the class, standing outside the classroom, sitting between two girls, facing the trash bin or running around the playing field. The classroom has one more feature that carries over to work life and the corporate world. The classroom does not allow dialogue between a teacher and a student. Most children are not supposed to ask questions to the teacher. If that were permitted, imagine the chaos and the queries with which the teacher might get flooded, immensely delaying the curricular schedule. A student asking too many questions in public is considered to be slow and stupid by the teacher and fellow students. Teacher would ask such student to study with full attention at home. So it is better to stay quiet and seek clarification later on with friends or parents. Mostly, the practice of asking questions to someone elder or senior is also taken as questioning their knowledge and authority, which can attract the wrong kind of attention.

Children are no less than devils. They come prepared with tricks learnt from the Bollywood movies. Playing innocent, many times they do ask questions in the classroom to test the teacher or to pass the time in a boring subject. Also, teachers who refer to a book in the classroom are not credited with understanding and wisdom. Children would negatively judge that teacher as 'just reading from the book'.

Schools are where parents undergo stress test.

Schools in India also slice the country in a peculiar way. There are some schools which are for children of elites and rich. They plan to produce only the celebrity from celebrity kids. The other kind of schools is run by the Christian missionaries who impart education in English. The teachers in these schools can be of any religion though. They are considered to provide high standards of education with fluency in English. The other non-missionary run private schools are also the expensive ones, owned by neo-rich Indian business houses. They try to compete with highest international standards and claim to follow Ivy League universities of the west. At least that works very well for their marketing and equally justifies the exorbitant fee structure. The remaining private schools are run for economically struggling parents, who aspire for quality education standards but can be satisfied with the fancy name of the school. Many of them call themselves as public school. Meanwhile, religious groups also run their schools as charitable trusts. They too have children from all religions except for the Madrasas.

Most Indian schools are at least bilingual, preferably English being one of them.

To make it complicated, like many other things in India, the syllabus followed is up to the discretion of the school. Each state has its own syllabus and medium of education. They make state's official language as primary language of education and give choice for a second Indian language. Also there are national syllabuses offered both by the national government and private institutions. So, a school is at liberty to follow any syllabus and any medium. Government schools are the ones who trail behind their contemporaries in all aspects. They are nearly free, that also mean there could be one teacher for the grades and all subjects. The building might be a shed with little furniture.

All schools in India have uniform for their students. The number of different uniforms required for different days of the week, depends on the affluence. For sure, especially for boys, none of the schools, prescribe traditional Indian dress as their dressing code. Amazingly, most of them prescribe the classical British outfits like the neck tie, blazer, tunic and skirts. Britain's queen would be too pleased to know this fact.

Safety is for Dumb, to Secure is Smartness

In India the biggest protection against harm and injustice is one's connections to the rich and powerful. A connection is to know somebody higher up in the power structure of the country, and thereby stay protected while the common masses are exposed to insecurity. For example, the chauffeur of a high-ranking official would be almost as influential as his boss. He would be in demand to get things done.

Safety is not a practice because Indians think they are smart and 'know-it-all'

In health services, if you know the doctor or the nursing staff, you will receive better care, more attentive surgery and swifter medical attention. A rule book is just theoretical to an Indian, and talking about the law is often looked down upon. This means that it is pointless to demand a service as specified in a rule book. While driving, there is just one rule: save yourself. If you are able to stay safe by driving slower than the speed limit, or in the wrong lane, or even by running away after an accident, it is acceptable. By the time you are caught, things could have cooled down and one may be fine. There is a concept called 'compromise'. In the case of a non-fatal accident, both parties settle the claim after a mutual discussion.

When saving yourself on the road, the protection that you have in your hand is the horn. Blow horn as frequently as possible, to chase away devils on the road. It is not just a superstition, but a natural instinct that becomes inculcated in Indians. They have become addicted to blowing the horn periodically.

The best way to learn about authentic Indian driving behavior is to take a ride in an auto rickshaw. You would have already discovered more about the experience, in the book chapter "Auto Rickshaw".

Since it is legally mandatory to have vehicle insurance, people do have it, but Indians in their entrenched beliefs resent this sort of risk management product. Instead, they always have a picture of God, which they view as protection against any misfortune. There is hardly any market for home insurance policies against theft or fire. Spiritual chanting is the best insurance. The Hindu Swastika, or the number 786, or the Gods' images that feature on the main door frames are seen as enough to keep homes safe, in addition to three or four locks that ensure the owners a peaceful sleep. The local watchman is treated well to be extra vigilant when homeowners are away.

Anything valuable that needs protection is wrapped with a plastic cover. This could be TV remotes, mobile phones, suitcases, vegetables in the fridge, roofs, shoes, table tops, chair seats or even computer monitors and keyboards. There are even colorful fancy plastic covers for fridge tops, to protect them from scratches. Some use a plastic cover for their wallet, especially to protect against sweat and rain in the monsoon season, while others wrap high-value currency notes in a plastic sheet before stacking them into the safe. India is a cash-rich country and people prefer to transact in cash, even though it means carrying it in bags. So carrying plenty of cash is a way of life in India.

Women who are shopkeepers or street hawkers keep their cash safely folded inside a plastic cover, before tightly tucking it under their bra strap. It is an embarrassing scene when you make your shopping payments and wait for your change. You might want to look elsewhere while these ladies stick their hand inside their blouse and pull out that safely-hidden wallet to return your change. Before I met these street hawkers, I thought Bond girls were smart, keeping their hand guns tucked away in their pantyhose. In fact, a few million Indian women have already found that safe storage place in their lingerie.

On the construction site or factory shop floors, wearing helmets though mandatory is taken lightly as a rule. It is more of a convenience to carry loads on the head by the laborers than protection from the falling objects. Footwear and gloves for safety in factory or construction sites is seldom used. As the size of the business establishment decreases, so does the concept of safety.

> **As the size of the business establishment decreases, so does the concept of safety.**

Safety is not a practice because Indians think they are smart and 'know-it-all'. It is all left to the divine powers with the belief "whatever will be, will be". It is a common belief that when the time comes, even the best safety equipment will fail. You would be surprised to hear half a dozen instances where people had full gear on, still met with a fatal accident.

Safety is for dumb, to be secure is smartness.

T

- Toilets
- Travel Scams

Toilets

In India toilets facilities have not evolved as well as they have in the west. There are fewer toilets than what the population requires. In rural India, 70% of the population does not have toilets in their houses. With 53% of total population not having a toilet in their house, virtually every second person is defecating in the open. People can be seen lining up along the highways and railway tracks, during an early morning drive through the countryside. Most Indians do it squatting. They look like a large bird stalking the passer-by. For travelers to India, it is an important piece of useful information. Generally, though, toilets in a public area are not worth exploring. It is better to plan your stops, or hold it in until you find an appropriate place. Sanitation is a major issue across India.

Most toilets are suited to squatting pose. Like other aspects of India, the type of toilet divides the country. There are those who have a toilet in their homes, and those who do not. For the have-not's, the space behind a bush or on a farm are nature's spots. Those who have a toilet at home are further classified by those who have classical Indian toilets (which require squatting) and those who have a western-style WC. Like many other things, Indians like to copy and practice western features as an upgrade to their modernity and to elevate their status. My observations suggest that having a WC at home is one step up the Indian economic ladder.

Most interesting are the colors and the shades of the ceramics that are used to make both styles of toilet seats. The color could be red, brown, black, beige, pink, blue, grey and many others. It might deserve an entry into the record books for being so creative in making a poop pot.

One important point that travelers to India must note is that toilet paper is not used; instead there is a mug and water for the concluding act. It is therefore necessary to learn the use of the Indian-specific method when in India. The reverse is also true. Indians traveling abroad find it very difficult to cope with the practice of tissue paper. Large Indian corporations operating in the west have specialized training sessions to deal with this situation. Indians think a dry tail is dirty and not an effective toilet solution.

Travel Scams & Safe Travel

- Like all other tourist destinations in the world, India too has its share of travel scams. Some of them are trivial and can be avoided, while others can be malicious.

- Always pay for a taxi with smaller denominations first. Some are smart in swapping large denomination notes for smaller ones, so tourists end up paying double.

- Never accept any drink or food from co-passengers, especially if you are traveling alone. Tourists have been drugged and robbed.

- Always seek directions from a shopkeeper over the counter. They are more reliable and sincere in helping tourists.

- If booking through agents, check the ticket specifications such as date, time and class of travel. Air-conditioned coaches can just mean open windows.

- Always drink branded bottled water and check the seal and date.

- There are no weight restrictions for Indian railways. Anyone suggesting has to be dealt with suspicion.

- Apparels with international brands are readily available in roadside shops. Even though they may look genuine, it is a good chance that they are counterfeit.

- Always take a taxi or public transport from an authorized location. There are pre-paid taxi booths. If you can't find one, look for a queue of taxi or auto rickshaw. Those drivers who are soliciting and not in queue usually turn out to be frauds.

- Pricing could be higher for tourists if it is not a standard shop.

- In case, women feel uncomfortable in crowded trains or buses, they can avail 'women only' seats and coaches. It's the Indian idea of providing women's safety.

U

- Union of Indian States
- USA is aped - Britain is disliked

Union of Indian States

As of 2015, India as a country is made up of twenty-nine states (this keeps changing every couple of years) and each state has its own God, language, food, caste system, dialects, iconic leader and regional political parties. How Gods belong to a state, we have seen in the chapter 'Religion'. If anyone were to compare the states with Europe, India as a country could be called a Union of Indian States, like the European Union. As in Europe, the language between any two countries are very distinct in its phonetics and in its script too. The landscape is different and so is the dress. Similarly, in India, just by looking at a picture, one can differentiate the state where the dress belongs, especially what the ladies wear.

One has to be very careful in identifying the statehood of a person, because some Indians would not like to be identified with a particular state. The usual kind of English, Welsh and Scottish rivalry prevails in India too.

The state of Bihar is also known as the state of large-scale corruption. People from Bihar are called *Biharis*. Although they are as hard-working as any other citizens of India, addressing someone as *Bihari* can be derogatory.

All North Indians are not Biharis

Similarly, the state of Punjab has Sikhs as its population. They are called *Sardars*. One of the most prosperous states in the country, its natives is identified by the wearing of a turban. This community, although considered as a separate religious sect by name, is also known for entrepreneurship, farming capabilities, and lightheartedness. The success of the extensive Indian road transport system and to great extent small and medium businesses is also attributed to this community. In social terms, all great Indian jokes have a Sikh as a central funny 'moron'. These days this funny *Sardar* is replaced by the more hilarious set of characters from the same community like 'Santa and Banta'. The duo of *Santa and Banta* has beaten the intelligence norms. They have even asked for multiple passwords for the same login because the reverse is true.

Until some time ago, all Indians living in the southern states and eating rice were referred to as *Madrasi*. This is because Madras, now Chennai was the most identified city in South India and South Indian states are primarily rice-eating states. In common parlance, they were called *Madrasi*. This also alerts us that not all those living in the southern states of India are *Madrasis*.

I am calling it a 'Union of Indian States' because each state, although characteristically different, still has common characteristics of India. Hence my objective of writing this book, to show the world the diversity within the commonality of India.

Crossing from one state to another is as easy as driving or flying in, but the characteristic condition of the roads and traffic are characteristics of the state. People usually talk about the road conditions to identify a particular state. For example, the state of Gujarat is known for excellent roads, while there are other states where it is difficult to find a road between potholes. In fact, the states can also be identified by the length of time, electricity run in the homes. The duration can be a few hours of daily load-shedding or a few hours of supply in total. Even the national capital of India, Delhi, and the commercial capital Mumbai do not have uninterrupted power supplies.

India is like a union because the Indians never miss an opportunity to get them photographed proudly with costumes of the different states and to demonstrate the country's unity in diversity. All cinema halls play the national anthem before the start of the movie, although the audience does not bother to follow the expected courtesy. The Union of India comes together twice in a year in a show of solidarity, as one nation. This happens on Republic Day, which is on 26th January, and again on 15th August, which is Independence Day. On all other days, it is the patriotic movie, a terrorist attack, or the cricket team's performance which binds the union together.

Although the number of states in India is twenty-nine at the moment, the numbers keep on increasing. The effect of this movement is that most Indians have lost count of the number of states. You would seldom come across an Indian who has kept count. Also, the number does not matter much to an Indian, because it is neither an exam question, nor a question in a job interview.

The number of states in India keeps changing; hence Indians don't keep a count now

The British have thankfully united the states of India, and most of the Indian bureaucracy like the parliament, the postal service, the railways, the water department and the roads can all be attributed to them. Reminiscence can still be seen, where the judicial system and the governments work exactly as their British equivalents.

Many streets and places still continue to be named after prominent figures of the British Empire. Some time ago, in a wave of nationalism, some cities were renamed, such as Bombay becoming Mumbai, Madras becoming Chennai, Bangalore renamed Bangaluru and Calcutta changed to Kolkatta.

USA is aped - Britain is disliked

Indians are more fascinated by US than any other country on the planet. People like to emulate the Hollywood stars and appreciate the country's position as a world superpower. Politically, India had been closer to Russia in terms of technological and military cooperation, still there are more Indians settled in the US than in Russia. Living in the US brings premium to an Indian's status. Further, talking and practicing the US style management in Indian corporate is considered as being modern and forward looking.

All students aspire to be educated in a US university and if not, would like to find work in the US after graduating. Any institution will find credibility if they are associated, certified by any agency or institution of the United States. American coffee and fast food chains are a craze and every time an outlet opens in a neighborhood, it definitely makes news. Automatically, they also become a landmark when seeking driving directions. Prospective grooms living and working in US are more sought after than those remaining one in India. A US brand, even though made in China is an acceptable addition to one's status. Attempt to speak in American accent is always welcomed and college campus can be spotted with numerous imitations of Americans' wearing, speaking and listening to music as if they were in the US.

The only sticky point with US is their support for India's arch enemy, Pakistan. Every news item which moves US away from Pakistan is welcomed in India. Only if US lawmakers realize that they will be welcomed in India most warmly, if they just overfly India's western neighbor.

Britain on the other hand is held responsible for the current plight and poverty of India. Indians have been subjects of the British and they still possess the Indian 'Kohinoor' diamond. Every child in their single digit age wants to get his Kohinoor back from Britain. Someone from UK government reading this book must understand that winning the Indian heart is conditional to simply returning their "Kohinoor', even though for a current market price.

V

- Vegetarianism
- Villages

Vegetarianism

Even though it might look very simple, vegetarianism and its practice are very confusing and complex, especially in the context of Indians. The four main religions of India have different interpretations of vegetarianism; for example, Muslims, Christians, Hindus and Sikhs are mostly non-vegetarians, but there can be days in a week when they are vegetarian. We will come to know about these variations a bit later. Before that we need to understand the concept of vegetarianism, rather than the word itself. Remember, in any conversation with Indians, all non-vegetarian food is called 'meat' in India.

To start with, there are only two types of eating habits that prevail. They divide the country's population into vegetarians and non-vegetarians. Those who practice vegetarianism make it less for reasons of diet, allergy or cruelty to animals and more for religious compliance. They have been brought up in that environment since childhood.

Often, non-vegetarians in the west are confused between vegetarian foods and animal products, such as dairy products and eggs. Well, Indian vegetarians approve of milk, butter and cheese, but not eggs. Though many vegetarians may eat birthday cakes and biscuits as a courtesy to the hosts, yet they do not consume cooked eggs such as in omelets or hard-boiled.

Welcome to the complexity which has already begun here.

There are many who are called vegetarians, but with terms and conditions. The Jain vegetarians and many others like them are strictest in their definition of vegetarianism. They cannot touch any non-vegetarian food like meat or fish, or bring any item of a similar kind into their home, including those made of eggs. In addition, they also do not eat root vegetables like peanuts, onions and garlic, which are also prohibited in Jain vegetarianism.

I wanted to know how these vegetarians survive, and if they do, are they all size zero? To my amazement, not only do they survive, they live longer than average and can be obese too. You will find a table at the end of this chapter, to help simplify the complexity of vegetarianism in India. Please keep this table handy if you are hosting or being invited by an Indian.

The cow is considered to be holy, likened to a mother hence they are worshipped and can never be killed for food. In fact, if you are discussing your western cuisine with Indians, especially with those aged fifty or more, avoid talking about your beef and pork dishes. Not only will the discussion come to an abrupt end, after you leave they will probably have to sprinkle holy water from the river Ganges on the place you were sitting. Some strict ones would not even like to pronounce the word 'meat', let alone dine at the same table where it is being eaten.

For Hindus and Sikhs, milk is considered auspicious and a sign of purity. According to Hindu mythology, it was the favorite food of Lord Krishna, the most powerful of all Hindu Gods. He can be identified as a God playing a flute, beside a holy cow. Because milk represents purity, all Hindus, Sikh and Jain rituals include extensive use of cow's milk. The deities are bathed in milk before worship and their shrines are washed with cow's milk. Most Indians are not 'Vegans'.

On the other hand, Indian milk is also a measure of honesty in Indian society. The milkmen, like those in the UK in the 1960s and 1970s, are usually small household businesses and have found tricks to boost their income; adding water to their milk is the most common one. Since the milk is delivered every day to a family, it is common practice for women to question the milkman about the quality of milk from the previous day. They warn of deductions from the monthly bill if they find the milk short of cream.

Early morning is the time of the milk delivery because it is sold when fresh, unlike in the supermarkets, where it is pasteurized and stored for days on end. If you are living in India, chances are you will be woken up by a milkman every morning for the measuring and receiving of milk in your personal container. Also, the entire country buys milk on a month's credit.

Being a Jain vegetarian or some other stricter vegetarians also means that you cannot eat onions and garlic. These are foods considered to have a tendency to disturb one's calm temperament and therefore they are considered as 'must be avoided'. Being vegetarian also means that even the cooking oil used once for frying non-vegetarian items cannot be re-used for cooking vegetarian food. Hence, in India, you will find plenty of restaurants which are called 'Pure Vegetarian'. Jains also do not eat any vegetable that is grown under the ground.

If you have noticed, while standing in the queue for a Subway® sandwich, very often an Indian will ask the server to change their gloves. He would have observed that a previously served sandwich had non-vegetarian ingredients. Often, I have seen staff serving in the fast-food shops asking an Indian customer just to remove the meat from their food, to make it vegetarian. Only, if it was as simple as that.

Fish is considered a vegetarian food in some coastal parts of India, but is usually considered non-vegetarian. While a Hindu non-vegetarian can eat goat meat, chicken and fish, beef and pork are prohibited. Muslims, who are mostly non-vegetarian, can have beef but definitely avoid pork.

The level of strictness can vary. Some non-vegetarians are strict vegetarians on Tuesdays, Saturdays, on days of festivals, when their wives are pregnant or when someone is critically ill. Other vegetarians eat cake only at birthday parties to honor their hosts, but would never bake one at home. In the significant state of Gujarat, selling meat and fish in the open display market is prohibited.

Interestingly, alcohol is loosely connected with vegetarianism, as some vegetarians are also teetotalers. This may be due to the fact that those restaurants serving alcohol also serve non-vegetarian food.

Indians have devised a method in case there is a combined buffet for a modern Indian social gathering. The demarcation is made with the rice dish. Please check with your local host about the order in which the dishes are placed on a buffet table, in case they are not labeled. It is considered that labeling is rude and over-formal etiquette. Also, Indians are usually experts in recognizing the dishes by observation rather than reading the labels below, so it would be regarded as patronizing the guests to do so. If there are labels, very often you will find them illegible as someone has already spilled curry and gravy over them. For large buffets, it is expected that there is a server per dish to inform you about the ingredients and serve you the food onto your plate. Please refer to the following table to know more about the type of Hindus and complicated 'vegetarianism' of India.

VEGETARIANISM - WHO CAN EAT WHAT

	Vegetarians	Non-Vegetarians	Milk	Eggs	Fish	Chicken	Goat Meat	Beef	Pork	Onion/Garlic	Alcohol	Tobacco
HINDUS (1)	✓	✗	✓	✗	✗	✗	✗	✗	✗	✗	✓	✓
HINDUS (2)	✓	✗	✓	✗	✗	✗	✗	✗	✗	✓	✓	✓
HINDUS (3)	✗	✓	✓	✓	✓	✓	✓	✗	✗	✓	✓	✓
MUSLIMS	✗	✓	✓	✓	✓	✓	✓	✓	✗	✓	✗	✓
CHRISTIANS	✗	✓	✓	✓	✓	✓	✓	✗	✗	✓	✓	✓
SIKHS	✗	✓	✓	✓	✓	✓	✓	✗	✗	✓	✓	✗
JAINS	✓	✗	✓	✗	✗	✗	✗	✗	✗	✗	✗	✗

Villages

The term 'village' can be used interchangeably for economically poor and administratively neglected places in India. This would mean a disrupted power supply, negligible medical services, broken roads, poor sanitation, a water supply in disarray and a primary school with one or two teachers at best. Probably villagers have to walk some distance from their homes to get water. There are nearly half a million villages in India and some of them still do not have power connected. So it is as if they have been camping forever.

It is important to know the definition of a village in India because if you say you live in a village in a western country, or would like to spend your retirement there, then Indians might downgrade your economic status by a catastrophic number of points.

In the Hindi language, calling someone a 'villager' means illiterate and rowdy, this is not always the case in real life though. Like all other countries in the world, the people of small towns are often more accommodating than the city guys. Since they are farm people, they do tend to have loud voices and less sophisticated. So, the term is more of a rhetoric metaphor than reality.

It is important to mention Bollywood here. All the lead characters are fascinated by those beautiful and innocent looking girls from the village. These girls in many movies are shown as vivacious, playful and flirtatious with the boy from the city, before other complications creep into the plot. They are clad in the most colorful dresses and even though the villages are supposed to be culturally conservative, the girl flashes four inches of cleavage. In real life, hundreds of these Bollywood movies are in no way accurate in this portrayal. One can hardly see any skin of a village woman. So when people across the seven seas watch those subtitled Bollywood movies, they should know the fact that Indian villages are way different from what is portrayed by Bollywood.

Many travelers want to visit Indian villages to get first-hand experience of their food, culture, clothing, folk music, songs and art. They are at the root of what is seen in the cities after being polished and commercialized. The other reason for visiting is the diversity in these villages. It is vast and immeasurable. It is a learning experience to see simple techniques used by the villagers when dealing with health care, maternity, quality of food, cooking methods and use of eco-friendly building material.

Of late, the villages of India have become popular among Indians living abroad. Parents who have migrated out of India and have children born and raised abroad travel with their children to Indian villages. They want to show their children the startling contrast between the two lifestyles. The idea is to keep kids grounded and not to get accustomed to comfort and ease. Whether this brief tourism is effective for this purpose, one cannot be really sure.

W

- Women Dressing
- Work Culture
- Weather and Time Zone

Women Dressing

Bangles and *Bindis* are an integral part of an Indian woman and must for a married woman. They have to wear them for the entire married life. Since color red is a sign of happy married life, it is required that women do wear some red bangles along with other colors and shades. For newlyweds, the bangles worn can be many, sometimes reaching up to the elbow. Subsequently, as years pass by, they can be reduced to a few, but must be enough to be prominently seen.

Bindis are the red dot that women wear in the middle of their forehead. Both married and unmarried women can wear it, but *Bindis*, along with vermilion filling the hair parting are a sign of a marriage, which they have to wear it till the end of their marriage. Every morning, before the ladies start their day, along with the prayers, these two signatures of marriage must be adorned. They also help attract respect and rightful position in the family and the society.

Hindu mythology has asked the women folk to be highly embellished with ornaments and with the best of attires. The decoration may not be the accurate translation. According to scriptures, women decoration and beautification is an art called *Shringar* and can positively transform the aura and motivation of the household. There are volumes of scriptures, music and dance forms in India, which is enhancing the concept of women beautification and its consequences. When talking about women beautification as described in Indian classical literature, it is not to be misread as glamour. *Shringar* is a symbol of femininity and fertility as linked with the Goddess Lakshmi, who is the goddess of beauty, fertility and prosperity in the Hindu culture. The literature indicates how women used to adorn themselves from tip to toe using jewelry and makeup to make their husbands happy when they came home after a long day of work. This was a mechanism to comfort their husbands by taking their attention away from the stress they have had.

In modern times, if there is another topic about India which is very confusing. It is about women's dressing. Before any guides suggest the kind of dress suitable for ladies, it is important to know what this confusion is all about. Even though I have lived in India for a long time, I am unable to find a defining principle for women's dressing.

All states have their own traditional dress, and lately the fashion industry moved dramatically from one view to another in defining fashion. Sometimes it is gaudy dresses with heavy jewelry, other times it is backless tops. Do they define classical Indian dressing stereotype? The answer is, maybe.

Sometimes western dress as simple as jeans, pants or a long-sleeved shirt can attract criticism, while on the other hand a revealing short Indian traditional *saree* can be welcomed. If measured by the square inches of skin exposed, a typical Indian woman in a *saree* is revealing more than any other female wearing jeans and a shirt or a western-style gown for that matter. *Sarees* have an open midriff all around the waist of the lady. The blouses too have a low neckline and the back can be deep. In fact, in the state of Gujarat, the regular blouses are backless, tied with a couple of strings to hold together the frontal structure.

Many traditional women's dresses, like the *lehenga*, a kind of long skirt with extraordinary frills, are tied on the navel or below. The *choli* comes down from the shoulder top, but is far too short to join the skirt. Even though there is a perception that Indian society is well-dressed, clothes cover much less than a woman's entire body surface area.

With this entire skin showing in *sarees*, the dress which covers the maximum is the one originating from the state of Punjab, called *salwaar kameez*. It is like a long shirt dress reaching the knees, the *Salwar*, with a loose *pajama* bottom. Even if it covers completely, the dress is seen as inappropriate if the girl fails to wear a *chunni*, a type of long scarf, to camouflage the curves of the breast. On one hand, there are revealing dresses that Indian society accepts, while on the other hand a concealing outfit has to have an additional cover. Therefore, revealing and concealing does not necessarily classify the appropriateness of Indian women's dressing.

All Indian festivals and family occasions like birthdays, engagements, and marriages require women to wear their traditional dress. It can be concluded that women, if they wear their traditional dress, however revealing it may be, are seen as acceptable. But wearing any western dress, including a pair of jeans or a full sleeve floor length evening gown is looked upon as inappropriate or excessively modern and sexually inviting. Why?

Whenever Indian movie directors want to portray a vamp, prostitute or a character with low morals, the female is dressed in a western gown with thigh high slit, a glass of wine and cigarette. So, there is a perception created to correlate the western outfit with sluts and women of low morals. The reason is Bollywood again that has made its mark.

Work Culture – Chalta Hai

Indian work culture is an art in itself. Whether it is about constructing a mega building, running Indian railways or creating a website, the characteristic signature of being 'Made in India' boldly reflects. Tall building may house hundreds of flourishing offices and businesses, but may have poor parking facilities. Probably the approach to the building may have a broken footpath. The airline would run on time, but the ground staff may be discourteous. The railways would carry a dozen million people but have stinking toilets and filthy stations. There are numerous similar examples which suggest that Indians are at work here.

The Indian attitude is casual, towards most things conducted as official.

Indians sparingly use the right tools. A motor mechanic, an electrician, plumber can solve most issues with only a monkey wrench, a screwdriver and a test bulb. Often you will find that there is a set of washers and screws remaining when the machine has been reassembled after the repair. The washer in the nut-bolt combination is a redundant component, according to an Indian workman.

The first mile and last mile problem reflects in all the Indian assets too. They will take you there; serve the purpose, but nothing like the quality standards as seen in the developed countries.

It is a saying that Indian project planning (the first mile) is considered as a waste of time and unessential. Too much deliberation only reduces the enthusiasm of doing the "thing". Indians want to do things, try new things even if they are done in a wrong way. Similarly, the finishing (the last mile) is a big issue. Indians are heard everywhere talking about *chalta hai*. This means, why worry about the aesthetics and fine touches, when it works without it. It is more important that the purpose is served, rest everything is a luxury.

Few examples can be quoted here. The Indian wholesale markets, whichever the city is, they are the most chaotic ones. The alleys are narrow and they get narrower because of encroachment. The streets would be dirty with least traffic regulation and clouded with overhead electricity wires. Still, it is flooded with traders and customers because it is cheap. It is serving the Indian purpose. In case, someone complains about the state of affairs and shopping experience, people show the direction to those air-conditioned malls where the prices are exorbitant. Hence, Indians buy from the wholesale markets, but enjoy the ambiance of the shopping malls.

Only 90% of things work well in India!

During Obama's visit to India in 2015, as chief guest of the prestigious and grand Republic Day parade, the Indians managed to provide a bulletproof enclosure which was not weather proof though. Poor American guest had to take the cold winter shower of Delhi for an hour or so. Only if the organizers had checked the weather report the previous night, they would have prepared accordingly.

Even with so much of attention and importance, only 90% of things work well in India!

Weather and Time Zone

The weather is nothing like the Bollywood drama. Rather, there is no drama in it. For the reason that the weather changes only three or four times a year, talking about the weather is not a conversation starter. For Indians, weather and climate are synonymous. Indians traveling abroad are surprised by the frequent weather reports and shocked to find a dedicated TV channel. According to them, a weather report means just the minimum and maximum temperatures for some fifteen cities of India. The weatherman of India could go on a long leave after publishing the weather forecast for the next month.

When it is cold, there is snow and ice in the northern part of India. Where there is none, it is cold with temperature hovering around freezing. It is colder for Indians because the homes are not heated well and floors are not carpeted to insulate. Hence, Indians rely only on heavy blankets and woolen clothing throughout the winters. Moreover, the doors and windows are not airtight, leaving the chill creeping through the gaps throughout the season. So winters are always present in the bedroom and bathrooms.

The south of India is mild during winters with temperatures around mid-twenties in the day making them ideal for getaways and holidaying.

Come summers, which peaks during mid-June, the national capital can touch forty-five degrees Celsius and above. It does not mean the city is not moving. It is still at its pace and the rush peaks in the evening when Indians go out to the nearest park with their families for dinner picnics. Summers in coastal cities are very humid, therefore sweaty. If people are not residents, they travel to the city only if necessary.

Though nature provides for four seasons, India claims to have three. The third is the monsoon, which touches the southern state of Kerala, typically on first June, every year. The it makes its way up to the Himalayas. The nation is washed with heavy rains for a month or so which easily disrupts air, road and rail traffic. The newspaper editors get themselves ready to get dramatic pictures of flooded city streets

A-Z Dealing with Indians

and children playing in the muddy waters. The government embraces itself for tackling floods and devastations in at least couple of states. Floods in the state of Assam are a regular feature and it would be a surprise if there is none in a year.

Leaking roofs are a regular feature and Indians are experts in using a variety of kitchen utensils and other containers to collect dripping water. Even the new built houses have this unique feature of getting mild to heavy leakages. It creates an artistic patch of mold and dampness after the monsoons have left India. I would guarantee if there is any house in India, which does not develop dampness during the monsoons. There must be a corner which has to have a stamp of the great Indian monsoon or let's say the great Indian builders. Since repainting the house is expensive and cumbersome, it is not done every year. Hence the patches are a constant reminder of the third Indian season.

Frogs and snakes make their way onto the Indian streets in the monsoon. The snakes, which they are a lot, owing to their poisonous fangs, get chased away or killed by the scared Indians. The frog skin makes up for the leather coating of the Indian roads where vehicular traffic is really brutal to these innocent ones. Otherwise, the stillness and silence of the neighborhood are broken by the croaking frogs and numerous insects that cloud anything that is illuminated. Typically, all Indian lamp shades have a dark patch which signifies the load of dead monsoon flying insects filling up the lamp bowl. Even the televisions are not spared. People get a load of dead insects from inside their blown up TV sets which usually get repaired for a couple of dollars in the local market.

Indian Standard Time (IST) is also called Indian Stretchable Time because timeliness is scarce in India

The time zone is unique. It is Indian Standard Time (IST +4:30 GMT in summer time). It is also called 'Indian Stretchable Time', because timeliness is scarce in India and time is in abundance. It does not have the feature of DST. So the flights coming from the west during summers reach an hour later than in the winters. This makes the referencing with other countries a bit complicated.

DST also provides an excuse for Indians being late for a meeting with international partners, in case they have run out of other excusable ideas.

For those Indians who are travelling to the west and far west for the first time, DST seems to be an amazing concept. It is something which they do relay it back home for the natives to be amazed. The amazement comes with an obvious questions of time management and its compliance by the entire population of a country. When compared to India, where time management is never accurate or precise, but delivered in a range of hours, days or weeks, Indians getting amazed with the concept of DST. How the entire population in millions are changing their clocks twice a year, is beyond imagination. The families of Indians living abroad continue to ask "so what time is it there now?" even when they have been talking about the subject for past 5 years.

X

- Xclusive Shopping List for foreigners

Xclusive Shopping List for foreigners

- Custom-tailored suits
- Hand-made shoes and sandals
- Incense sticks
- Infused tea or herbal tea
- Spices
- Ladies fashion accessories
- Bangles, Ear rings and Nose pins
- Pashmina Scarf and Shawl
- Prescription glasses
- Dental work
- Straw Yoga mat and a Yoga book
- Yoga bag
- Snacks and Savories
- Wooden handicraft
- Silk clothing
- Woolen carpet

Y

- Yoga

Yoga

Though a chapter on Yoga comes towards the end of this book by virtue of it trailing alphabetically, Indian cannot be complete without Yoga. It is that part of lifestyle which all Indians proudly own and practice. So much so, that they all consider themselves an expert. Their body weight and figure might speak contrary to their expertise.

Yoga is a household name and every Indian owns a version of it. While it is the long term solution to the health, Indians do recommend yoga for all ailments. Over a period, Ayurveda, the Indian form of medicine, has got blurred with the practice of yoga. The wider understanding in India is that both make a very powerful mix for well-being and healthy longevity.

The glamour still lies with the gyms and jogging parks in India with Lycra® and body hugging dresses. Yoga has to grow few dozen points to be glamorous. Few reasons are: one, because Indians usually practice it with loose Pajamas and secondly, it is mostly the mature ones who are found to be doing it. While walking in the park, the chances are that a beautiful, sleek girl might whiz past you in smart jogging tracks while some heavy ones in their night dress would be lying on the grass, trying their best to entangle themselves in a yoga pose.

> **All Indians consider themselves an expert in Yoga, including myself. Though the body weight and figure may signify differently.**

While the west has been innovative in defining different forms of yoga, including the Iyengar Yoga and Hot Yoga, most in India stick to conventional home-style practice. According to them, theirs is the best one while that in the west is more of an exercise than spirituality.

Z

- Zoo – We live here

Zoo – We live here

On average, an Indian co-exists with a far larger number of animals than any other humans from the developed world. Many of them are so much part of Indian life that they are not even considered different from the human species. So, lets describe them all in the descending order of their size.

Someone traveling on roads is bound to meet a cow, a buffalo, a goat or a dog. This is not in a rural area, but common also in big towns. Cows might be found sitting on a street corner, so that traffic has to make its way past them. It is only in circumstances when the road gets blocked because of an oblivious animal, that humans intervene to shoo them into another corner. It is to make just enough room for the traffic to keep moving. Also common is for cows to snatch vegetables from a vendor's shop or kiosk. All that one does is to shoo them away and thereafter it is business as usual. The same happens with buffalo and goats, who can roam about freely in the streets like any other honorable citizen of India.

In many cities, it is common to see large sized cows being fed respectfully by passers-by. The owners of these cows anchor them near a busy street or near the financial district. The happy animal munches on the green grass duly fed, while its owner gets tips for bringing a good luck charm to the location. Readers could see this as a business, but this is not how Indians look at it. Feeding the cows in the morning is supposed to bring good luck in business and remove bad omens. Woman of the house makes the first *Roti* (Indian Bread) for the cow, which the husband carries while going to work. He feeds any cow seen first on the road.

Horse-drawn carriages are also sighted frequently, mostly in the old part of historical cities. They carry people from place to place. Most of the time they are used as a means of intra-city transport, in areas around the railway and bus stations. As primitive as it may sound, they do make a pleasant journey through the town, especially when most of the charioteers are friendly and chatty. Not only do they talk to their passengers, but they also keep talking to their horses. Sometimes, you might answer a question which was actually not meant for you.

Donkeys are commonly found in areas of building construction where they carry loads on their back. Also, the mule finds a use in the hilly areas of India, where they carry tourists to places of pleasure and religion. Some famous places of pilgrimage such as *Vaishno Devi*, where the highly respected Goddess for Hindus resides, are accessible only by a mule ride. This is to negotiate steep hilly tracks leading up to the destination.

Camels are a frequent sight in the northern states of Gujarat, Rajasthan and Haryana for the purpose of transport through the arid desert terrains. In fact, camel milk is regularly consumed in these states and is considered to have medicinal properties. As I discovered, camel milk is loaded with more nutritional value than cow's milk. But in India, this message is not promoted and no one wants to know more about this remarkable animal. The cow will remain the most sacred animal.

Indian elephants are favorites and participate in religious festivals. They attract extraordinary attention from the public, who treat them with reverence and amazement. The owners of the elephants (*mahout*) roam about in the cities, walking up to people and visiting shops and schools to ask for charity. In return, donors get to touch the trunk of the elephant on their forehead, as a mark of blessing from the God *Ganesha*. It is auspicious, and a very big deal in India. In the southern state of Kerala, one can participate in a grand elephant parade. The elephants are richly decorated with gold ornaments on the occasion of festivals.

Houses are also no strangers to wildlife and members of the animal kingdom. Household lizards are common and their favorite hiding places are behind wall clocks and hanging pictures. More often they are seen sticking to the wall like a painting, waiting for their prey or resting peacefully after a good catch. The life of the humans in that room just continues as usual. At the most, people cover their food in order to prevent the reptiles nesting in there. You might be watching your favorite sitcom and behind the television could appear a lizard, few inches long, stuck on the wall. Indians are not at all frightened of lizards. On the contrary, lizards get frightened by the loud humans in those television programs.

Spiders, red ants and black ants are also very common. Clearing spider webs from the corners of the room is at least a weekly activity one has to undertake.

> **Indians are perpetually in a state of high alertness. They can switch to fire-fighting and problem-solving mode with great ease.**

It is a way to check if the cleaning is meticulously done or not. Finding a spider web in a corner can discount the payments agreed for cleaning services. Spiders and ants are never killed, because they are considered saviors in Islam. The belief has caught on with the whole of India. One might be surprised to find ants even on the very high floors of an apartment building too. If sugar or sweets are left out in the open, ants in large numbers are your guests. Ladies at home struggle with ants and cockroaches all through their work life, covering their dishes to protect them from one crawler or another.

There are more stray dogs on the streets of India than pets. Hence, it is advisable to be protective of yourself while walking past them. Although most of them are harmless, because of their health it is not advisable to let them come near you.

In the west, dog lovers are a significant community who can influence public behavior, laws and policies. The extent to which western dog-lovers spend money and take care of their pets can be overwhelming and at times shocking to Indians. It would not be appreciated in India because of the economic conditions and the general understanding of dogs as animals. Calling someone a 'dog' is highly derogatory. It is considered pretentious to be a dog lover and to spend a fortune on dogs by Indian standards is termed crazy. It is a developing society, one must understand.

There are mosquitoes and flies a-plenty. Especially in the monsoon season, which lasts from June until August, these miniature animals are a menace. There are methods to drive them away, but if someone does not know what a nuisance, they are, it will be very irritating and frustrating. People can suffer from lack of concentration and lose sleep.

Ask an Indian if they were 'killing flies', rather than responding to your call. It would be the most apt and the harshest way of reprimanding someone for doing nothing.

Some Indian towns have a population of monkeys, who move around in groups from roof to roof, snatching drying clothes, swinging on the antenna poles, basking in the sun after feasting on stolen food, or just doing whatever pleases them. Those found in towns might be dangerous at times, so it is important to keep away.

Temples are other places where monkeys are found in all shapes and sizes. Unlike the ones found in the towns, they are very friendly and can predict human behavior intelligently. They are fed as a religious practice by pilgrims, with food which can be bought from local shops. So there is an expectation about the animal kingdom which all humans visiting the temple must fulfill. Talking about monkeys, there are local breeds that vary from place to place. Feeding the monkeys at religious locations is understood to bring good omens. *Hanuman*, the God who resolved another senior God's crisis, is assumed to protect and resolve the problems of his devotees. This is why the monkeys in India, especially at religious places, enjoy the privileges that they do.

It will come as no surprise that India is the land of snake charmers. There are plenty of snakes of different types found in India. With a light drizzle, they all come out of hiding and can be spotted easily on the country roads. I am not sure how many of them are poisonous, but certainly the Indian King Cobra chills the spine of all Indians. They are long, up to six feet in length, spit venom which can blind, and their bite is fatal. They are called *Nag* in Hindu mythology and they appear to coil around the neck of the powerful God *Shiva*, like an outstanding ornament. Hence, the king Cobra is worshipped to please the Lord *Shiva*, the God of creation. On the fifth day of the bright lunar month of July or August, Hindus across the world offer milk and prayers to the snake deity *Nag*. There are dedicated temples and the idols are made of silver, stone or wood. People might come across snake charmers, who often roam the city on this day of the festival with a cobra in their baskets. They play typical *Nagin* (female snake) music on a pipe instrument called a *Been* to attract worshippers who are more than willing to make offerings in cash and kind.

How can Bollywood be left out when it comes to entertaining the population with the charm and grace of the Indian animal kingdom? There are blockbuster thriller movies with protagonist roles for horses, dogs, snakes and birds. In the case of snakes, the human reincarnation of male and female cobras as romantic couples has been portrayed. Much to the thrill of the audience, they could change their form from snakes to humans and back, in order to avenge the villains.

While Indians are dealing with these members of animal kingdom, in their daily lives, we have learnt something about "Dealing with Indians". It will take a life time to comprehensively explore the traits of an Indian, especially when they are in billions. But for now, it can be safely assumed that as a reader, we have made a good start.

Printed in Poland
by Amazon Fulfillment
Poland Sp. z o.o., Wrocław